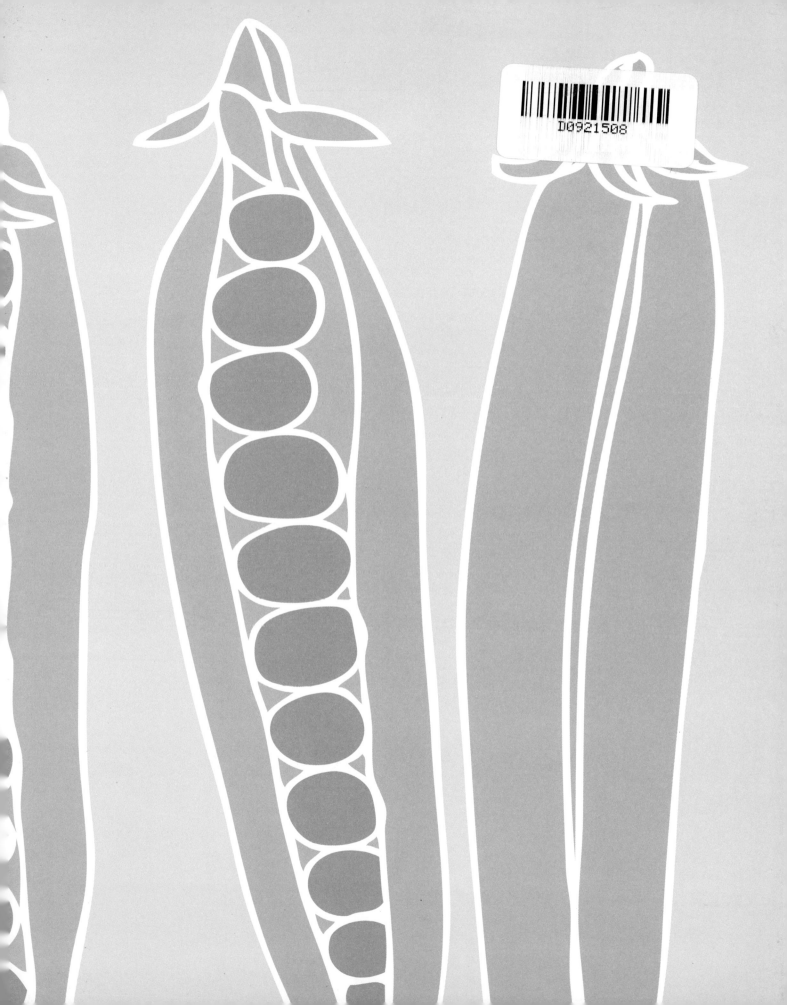

MARK
HIX
BRITISH
SEASONAL
FOOD

A
year round celebration
OF
the finest produce

PHOTOGRAPHY BY
JASON LOWE

QUADRILLE

In memory of
my father, Ernie

Publishing director
Jane O'Shea

Creative director
Helen Lewis

Project editor
Janet Illsley

Art direction & design
Lawrence Morton

Photographer
Jason Lowe

Illustrator
Marcus Oakley

Stylist
Cynthia Inions

Production
Marina Asenjo

First published in 2008 by
Quadrille Publishing Limited
Alhambra House
27-31 Charing Cross Road
London WC2H 0LS
www.quadrille.co.uk

Cataloguing in Publication Data:
a catalogue record for this book
is available from the British
Library.

ISBN: 978 184400 622 9

Printed in China

CONTENTS

Introduction

If, like me, you have a passion for well-sourced ingredients, cooking in season seems the obvious thing to do. I must admit that it can get a bit confusing these days with supermarkets stocking most vegetables and many fruits all the year round. But the great thing about cooking with British ingredients in their true season is that you really do enjoy them that much more. I don't want to be eating asparagus at Christmas or strawberries when it's snowing – I want to make the most of our homegrown produce at its best, however short the season. Cooking this way is satisfying and once the season is over I'm happy to wait till the following year to enjoy it once again.

I look on shopping as a source of inspiration – a fun thing to do, rather than a chore. I'd advise you not to plan menus too firmly before you actually go shopping, as you are more likely to be receptive to appealing produce that's just come into season. Buying on the hoof is not as difficult as you may think and is likely to make for much more varied meals.

Farmers' markets are always a stimulating place for me to buy food, because stallholders generally bring just what they've grown and produced. You'll also very often come across more interesting varieties of vegetables and fruits. The produce might not necessarily be cheaper than mass-produced imports, but you know that the money you are handing over is going directly to the farmer and not passed down through a chain where the producer at the bottom may receive a fraction of the price. Many farms sell direct by post as you can discover on the net, or you can visit farm shops for the real experience.

Foraging for herbs, mushrooms and hedgerow fruits is another way to appreciate the seasons and an enjoyable pastime. You will be surprised what a Sunday morning stroll with the kids can throw up... and it's all for free.

January

MALLARD *and other great feathered* game, Cornish CAULIFLOWERS *and tasty ways with* FISH BITS *that you won't have come across before...*

OTHER INGREDIENTS NOT TO BE MISSED

Pike   Turbot   Native oysters   Mutton   Pheasant   Partridge   Snipe   Woodcock

Parsnips   Swede   Jerusalem artichokes   Celeriac   Leeks   Cabbages   Greens   Salsify   Sprout tops

Pennywort   Hedgerow garlic   Velvet shank   Judas ear fungus

Forced rhubarb   Quince   Medlars

January could potentially be a dull month in the kitchen, but I prefer to make it a bit of a culinary challenge – by bringing together everyday vegetables and other seasonal ingredients to make good wintry soups, casseroles and braises.

Now that Christmas and New Year celebrations are well out of the way we can get our cooking back in order. It's not that I mind a fridge full of food, but in some ways it is a relief to get back to normal – and rather more stimulating to have a bit of seasonal minimalism in the house…

As there is still some game around now, why not have a bit of a game feast to remember it by until later on in the year?

In particular, make the most of the wild duck family this month – widgeon, pintail, teal and mallard should all be readily available from good game merchants and in perfect eating condition.

As the feathered game season draws to a close around the end of the month, you'll find many butchers and game dealers will be almost giving the stuff away, so now is a good time to make a pie or casserole. Be careful though when you buy a game pie or casserole mix, as the various cuts will all have different cooking times. You may well end up with a dish that you expect to be lovely and tender, only to find tough bits in among the tender pieces.

There are two seasons for the good old British cauliflower: the winter variety, with the pick of the crop coming from Cornwall; and the summer cauli, more commonly grown in the North. Both have great flavours if they are cooked properly, but in the wrong hands cauliflower can turn into a watery mush. Lots of people think that cauliflowers – and most other vegetables for that matter – are just for boiling or covering with cheese sauce… well you'll be surprised.

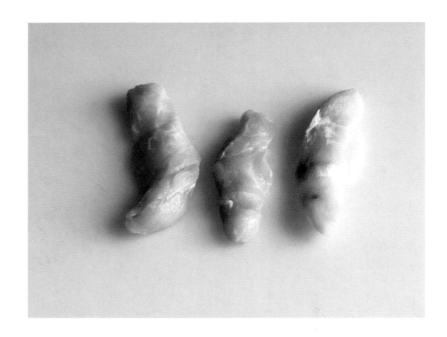

I've included a random section on fish bits this month too, because like many other cooks and food writers, I feel strongly that we are unconsciously depleting our fish stocks. It's not just about being aware of the species we are eating and their vulnerability, but also about making the most out of the fish we are eating on a regular basis.

Just how many of us make hearty soups at home with fish bones and heads, for example? And why don't fishmongers encourage us to use the cheeks and offal and other parts of the head, like the collars?

A walk around a Spanish or French fish market will give you a good idea of where I'm coming from. Alongside prime fish, like turbot and sea bass, you will see cod's tongues (illustrated above), skate cheeks and monkfish liver.

We have a similar problem with meat in that everyone tends to opt for the prime cuts, leaving the butcher with lots of the braising cuts, which are very tasty but generally end up going through the mincer. Cheaper cuts and odds and ends of meat and game can make very good eating in warming soups, casseroles and pies.

I will never forget an unusual fish dish I had in Spain some years ago – of salted cod's tripe with wild mushrooms. It was absolutely delicious. Those lovely gelatinous fish bits like the belly, collars and some intestines are surprisingly good and haven't got the strong taste of comparable cuts of meat.

A New Year's resolution to respect and make the most of our precious fish stocks really wouldn't go amiss.

Cauliflower

Cauliflower can be cooked in a variety of ways and its affinity with cheese increases the possibilities. Deep-fry blanched small florets that have been coated in breadcrumbs mixed with grated Cheddar. Or purée cooked cauliflower, spread in a gratin dish, top with breadcrumbs mixed with grated mature cheese and brown under the grill. Roasting intensifies the flavour of cauliflower and this is a great way to cook it – try it with meaty fish or offal.

Cauliflower florets also make ideal crudités to serve with an interesting dip alongside other veg dippers. And of course, piccalilli, one of my favourite pickles, is based on cauliflower.

However you cook it, timing is crucial with cauliflower. Whether it is in individual florets or whole, it needs to have a slight bite but be cooked right through.

CAULIFLOWER SOUP *serves 4–6*

This is an easy, economical soup to make and the flavour is excellent. You can finish the soup in various ways: blending in some grated mature Cheddar; or as you serve the soup dropping in some nuggets of blue cheese; or sprinkling in some cooked pearl barley, raisins and pine nuts, as the Italians do.

   1 small-medium cauliflower, dark outer leaves removed
   a good knob of butter
   1 medium onion, peeled and roughly chopped
   1 leek, white part only, trimmed, roughly chopped and washed
   1 litre vegetable stock
   500ml milk
   salt and freshly ground white pepper
   2–3 tablespoons double cream

Roughly chop the cauliflower and put to one side. Melt the butter in a pan and add the onion and leek. Put the lid on and cook, without colouring, for 3–4 minutes until soft.

Add the cauliflower, vegetable stock and milk. Season, bring to the boil and lower the heat. Simmer, covered, for 35 minutes or until the cauliflower is soft. Whiz in a blender until smooth, then strain through a fine sieve into a clean pan. Reheat gently, stir in the cream and serve.

CAULIFLOWER CHEESE *serves 4–6*

This is one of my all-time favourite dishes. It's great comfort food – perfect for family meals and TV suppers. Heads of cauliflower come in various sizes, some with more leaves than others. I prefer to keep and use the leaves in a dish like this – they taste great and give a bit of colour, so there's no point in wasting them.

   1 medium cauliflower
   1 litre milk
   ½ bay leaf
   salt and freshly ground black pepper
   60g butter
   60g plain flour
   100ml double cream
   120g mature Cheddar cheese, grated
   1–2 tablespoons finely chopped parsley

Cut the cauliflower into florets, reserving the leaves and stalk. Bring the milk to the boil in a saucepan, with the bay leaf added, and season well. Add the cauliflower florets and leaves, and simmer for about 7–8 minutes until tender. Drain in a colander over a bowl to reserve the milk.

Melt the butter in a heavy-based pan and stir in the flour. Stir over a low heat for about 30 seconds, then gradually stir in the reserved hot milk, using a whisk. Bring to a simmer and turn the heat down very low (use a heat diffuser if you have one). Continue to simmer very gently for 20 minutes, stirring every so often to ensure that the sauce doesn't catch on the bottom.

Add the cream and simmer for a couple of minutes. The sauce should be of a thick coating consistency by now; if not simmer for a little longer. Strain through a fine sieve into a bowl, whisk in three-quarters of the cheese, then taste and adjust the seasoning if necessary.

Preheat the oven to 220°C/gas 7 (or the grill to medium-high). Make sure the cauliflower is dry – you can use kitchen paper to pat it dry if necessary. Mix the cauliflower with half of the cheese sauce and transfer to an ovenproof dish. Spoon the rest of the sauce over and scatter the chopped parsley and the rest of the cheese on top. Either bake in the oven for about 20 minutes until golden, or reheat and brown under the grill.

ROAST CAULIFLOWER WITH DEVILLED LAMB'S KIDNEYS *serves 4*

Pan-roasting a thick slab of cauliflower is an ingenious way to serve it. Ray Driver, my old sous chef at Le Caprice, came up with the idea some years ago and it went down a treat. You can use a piece of cauliflower like this as a base for all sorts of meaty dishes, but I reckon its caramelised sweetness is best suited to offal.

1 small cauliflower, trimmed

salt and freshly ground black pepper

100g butter

plain flour for dusting

14 lamb's kidneys, halved and trimmed

FOR THE SAUCE

4 shallots, peeled and finely chopped

6–10 black peppercorns, coarsely crushed

a good pinch of cayenne pepper

3 tablespoons cider vinegar

3 tablespoons water

40g butter

2 teaspoons plain flour

200ml good beef stock

1 teaspoon English mustard

2 tablespoons double cream

8 small gherkins, finely chopped

Preheat the oven to 200°C/gas 6. Cook the cauliflower whole in boiling salted water for about 8 minutes. Drain in a colander, then place under cold running water for a few minutes until cool; drain well. Trim the ends from the cauliflower and cut into four 1½cm thick slices.

Melt half of the butter in a frying pan until foaming. Meanwhile, dust the cauliflower with flour and season well. Pan-fry, in two batches if necessary, over a high heat for a couple of minutes on each side until nicely coloured. Then place in the oven to finish cooking for 10 minutes (if your pan isn't ovenproof or big enough, transfer the cauliflower to a roasting pan).

Meanwhile, make the sauce. Put the chopped shallots, peppercorns and cayenne pepper in a saucepan with the cider vinegar and water. Simmer gently until the liquid has almost totally evaporated, then add the butter and stir in the flour. Gradually add the beef stock, stirring to avoid lumps forming. Season lightly with salt and pepper, and add the mustard. Simmer gently for 10–12 minutes. Add the cream and continue to simmer until the sauce is of a thick, gravy-like consistency. Add the gherkins and keep warm.

When ready to serve, season the kidneys. Melt the rest of the butter in a heavy-based frying pan. When hot, add the kidneys and cook over a high heat for a couple of minutes on each side, keeping them pink. Drain and add to the sauce. Simmer for 20 seconds or so.

Pat the cauliflower dry with some kitchen paper, then place a slab on each warm serving plate. Spoon the kidneys and sauce on top and serve straight away.

PICCALILLI *makes two 1 litre jars*

Most shop-bought piccalilli tastes far from good – usually because there are too many ingredients that just don't belong in the jar. Apart from the obvious things like hard cheeses and ham, piccalilli is great with potted ham, cold ox tongue, or even a hot pork pie.

1 small cucumber (or ½ large one)

1 small head of cauliflower

1 medium onion, peeled and diced

2 tablespoons fine sea salt

150g caster sugar

60g English mustard

1 teaspoon ground turmeric

1 red chilli, deseeded and finely chopped

280ml cider vinegar

20g cornflour

100ml water

Quarter the cucumber lengthways and scoop out the seeds, then cut into 1cm pieces. Cut the cauliflower into florets, halve each one and place in a dish with the cucumber and onion. Sprinkle over the salt and leave to stand for 1 hour.

Wash the vegetables well in cold water to remove excess salt and drain well in a colander.

Meanwhile, combine the sugar, mustard, turmeric, chilli and cider vinegar in a saucepan and bring to the boil. Lower the heat and simmer for 2–3 minutes. Mix the cornflour to a paste with the water, then whisk it into the liquor and continue to simmer gently for another 6–7 minutes, stirring continuously.

Tip the vegetables into a bowl, pour over the vinegar mixture and mix well, then transfer to sterilised jars. Seal and keep in a cool, dark place for up to 3 months. To store the piccalilli for longer (up to 6 months) immerse the jars in a pan of water before sealing and simmer for 15 minutes, then remove, cover and leave to cool.

Fish bits

'Save the cod' has been the motto of many food writers for some time, but the problem is that we are all guilty of urging each other to move on to a new species – making that vulnerable too. We need to diversify and concentrate less on the prime cuts. Cheeks, tongues, collars, monkfish livers, skate knobs and cod chitterlings (see left) are all tasty and deserve to be eaten. Most fish bits can be used in the same way as a piece of fish, or herring roes. Skate knobs, for example, are delicious breadcrumbed and deep-fried, as are monkfish cheeks.

FRIED MONKFISH LIVER WITH SWEET AND SOUR ALEXANDERS *serves 4 as a starter*

Alexanders grow along the roadsides and are prolific as you near the coastline in Kent. Somewhere between celery and cardoon, with a slightly perfumed taste, they can be treated in much the same way. You'll need to peel the stems first, then simply blanch, boil or braise them.

There is little demand for monkfish liver in the UK, so you'll probably need to ask your fishmonger to source it for you. For me, it's the foie gras of the fish world – it looks pretty similar and cooks up in much the same way.

8 stems of Alexanders, about 300–400g, trimmed, a handful of leaves reserved

salt and freshly ground black pepper

2 tablespoons extra virgin rapeseed oil

3 shallots, peeled, halved and finely chopped

4 tablespoons cider vinegar

2 tablespoons caster sugar

1 tablespoon tomato ketchup

1 teaspoon English mustard

100ml water

300–400g monkfish liver

a couple of good knobs of butter

Peel the Alexander stems and cut them into rough batons, about 5 x 1cm. Cook in boiling salted water for 3–4 minutes or until tender, then drain and leave to cool. Chop the leaves and set aside.

Meanwhile, heat the rapeseed oil in a pan and gently cook the shallots for a few minutes to soften. Add the cider vinegar, sugar, ketchup, mustard and water. Let bubble to reduce until there are just a few tablespoonfuls of liquor remaining. Stir in the Alexander batons and another splash of water. Season and simmer for a couple of minutes, then remove from the heat.

Cut the monkfish liver into 1cm thick slices and season with salt and pepper. Heat the butter in a heavy-based frying pan until foaming and cook the liver for a couple of minutes on each side until nicely coloured. Add the reserved Alexander leaves as you turn the liver to cook them briefly.

Spoon the Alexanders and sauce onto warm plates and top with the monkfish liver and wilted Alexander leaves. Serve at once.

COD CHITTERLINGS ON TOAST WITH
HEDGEROW GARLIC *serves 4 as a starter*

Cod chitterlings are the unformed roe of the cod and
take their name from pig's chitterlings, which they
resemble. You'll only find them for a couple of months
around now, and if your fishmonger can't get them for
you, then use herring roes instead. Hedgerow garlic,
which resembles garlic chives, can be used just like chives.
It has a much more subtle flavour than garlic.

400–450g cod chitterlings

about 300ml milk to cover

salt and freshly ground white pepper

150g butter

4 slices of bread, 1½ cm thick, cut from a
small bloomer-style loaf

handful of hedgerow garlic, washed, dried
and cut into large pieces

handful of capers, rinsed and drained

Rinse the chitterlings in cold water, then place in a
saucepan with the milk. Bring to the boil, lower the heat
and simmer for about 20 seconds, then set aside to cool in
the milk.

Drain and dry the chitterlings on kitchen paper and
season with salt and pepper. Heat 50g of the butter in a
non-stick or well-seasoned heavy-based frying pan and
cook the chitterlings over a medium heat for 4–5 minutes
until nicely coloured on all sides – they will curl up a
little during cooking.

Meanwhile, toast the bread. When the chitterlings are
ready, place a slice of toast on each warm plate and pile
them on top. Melt the rest of the butter in the pan, add
the chopped hedgerow garlic and capers, and stir over
the heat for a few seconds, then spoon over the roes.
Serve at once.

COD'S TONGUES WITH SMOKED PORK
BELLY *serves* 4 *as a starter*

Ok, the idea of eating cod's tongues might not appeal to everyone, but they have a delicious gelatinous quality about them, and can take on bold flavours, like smoked pork belly. If you're unable to find smoked belly, then buy a piece of smoked bacon instead.

200–250g smoked pork belly or smoked
bacon, in one piece

a couple of good knobs of butter

1 onion, peeled, halved and finely chopped

2 garlic cloves, peeled and crushed

1 teaspoon plain flour

100ml white wine

300ml fish stock

400g cod's tongues

salt and freshly ground black pepper

1 tablespoon chopped parsley

TO SERVE
4 slices of sourdough or country-style
bread, 1½cm thick

Cut the pork belly roughly into 1cm chunks. Heat half of the butter in a pan and gently cook the onion, garlic and pork belly for 3–4 minutes, turning every so often. Dust with the flour, stir well, then gradually stir in the wine and fish stock. Simmer gently for about 45 minutes.

Season the cod's tongues lightly with salt and pepper. Heat the rest of the butter in a frying pan and fry the cod's tongues over a high heat for 3–4 minutes until lightly coloured. Meanwhile, toast or griddle the bread on both sides.

Add the fried cod's tongues to the sauce, check the seasoning and scatter over the parsley. Place a slice of toast on each warm plate, spoon over the cod's tongues and sauce, then serve at once.

FISH COLLAR CURRY *serves 4–6*

I do enjoy a good fish head curry. When I worked at the Dorchester, the Bangladeshi kitchen porters would take all of our fish heads to make a delicious fish curry for their staff meals. There's a lot more meat left on the head of some of those larger species of fish than you might imagine.

I'm sure you're wondering what the collar is. Well, it's a meaty, gelatinous part of the fish around the back of the head where the gills are. It isn't really bony as such, but more of a plate structure surrounded by flesh.

Because the flesh is quite meaty, it stands up to a bit of rapid curry cooking and doesn't disintegrate in the way a fillet would. Ask your fishmonger to save you the collars from large fish like cod and halibut.

1.5kg fish collars

salt and freshly ground black pepper

60g ghee or vegetable oil

3 medium onions, peeled and roughly chopped

5 large garlic cloves, peeled and crushed

1 tablespoon chopped fresh root ginger

3 small, medium-strength chillies, deseeded and finely chopped

1 teaspoon cumin seeds

½ teaspoon fenugreek seeds

1 teaspoon fennel seeds

1 teaspoon mustard seeds

1 teaspoon cumin powder

½ teaspoon paprika

1 teaspoon ground turmeric

pinch of saffron strands

1 teaspoon curry powder

5 or 6 curry leaves

2 teaspoons tomato purée

juice of ½ lemon

1.3 litres fish stock (or a good stock cube dissolved in this amount of hot water)

3 tablespoons chopped coriander leaves

Season the fish with salt and pepper. Heat half of the ghee in a large, heavy-based pan and fry the pieces of fish over a high heat until lightly coloured. Remove with a slotted spoon and put to one side.

Add the rest of the ghee to the pan and fry the onions, garlic, ginger and chillies for a few minutes until they begin to soften. Add all of the spices, put the lid and cook for a couple of minutes to allow the spices to release their flavours, lifting the lid and stirring every so often.

Add the tomato purée, lemon juice and fish stock. Bring to the boil, lower the heat, season and simmer for 45 minutes. Take a cupful of sauce from the pan and whiz in a blender until smooth, then pour back into the sauce.

Add the pieces of fish and simmer for 15 minutes, then add the chopped coriander and simmer for a further 5 minutes. Taste and adjust the seasoning if necessary. Serve with basmati rice.

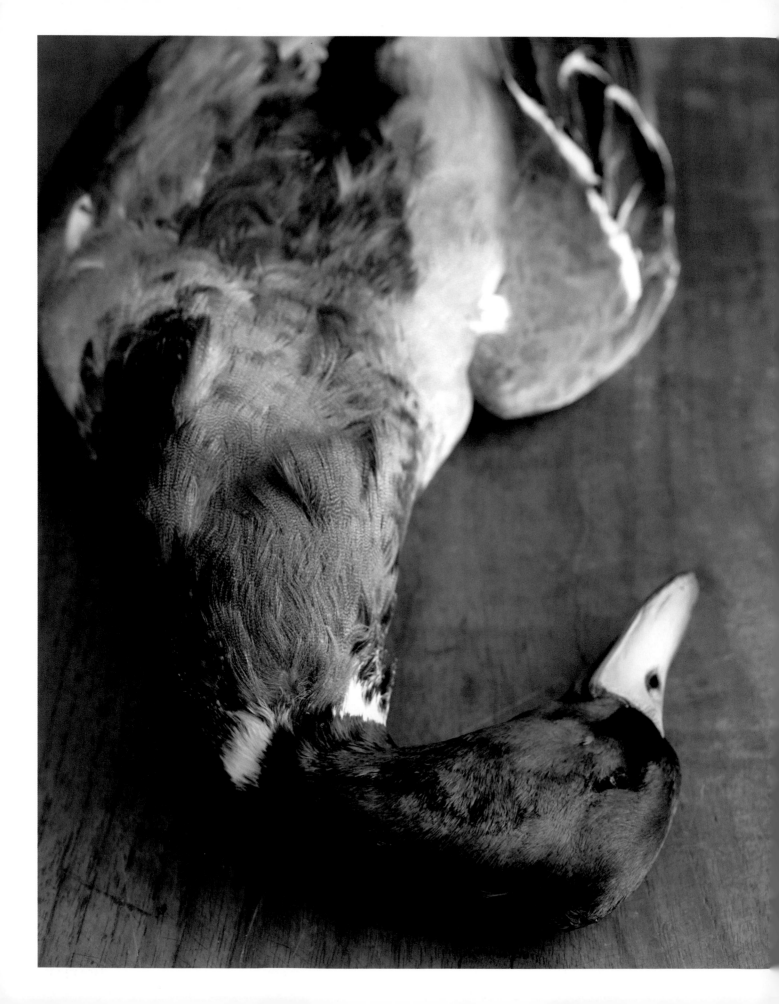

End of the game

Of all the game birds, I would say that the wild duck family are your best bet in this last month of the season. Mallard, pintail, widgeon and teal are all fattening up nicely and make good eating – accompanied by a simple tangy apple or quince sauce, or a rosehip jelly.

If you've been hoarding game birds in the freezer then why not make a hot pot or the faggots on page 23. Or you could turn them into a pâté or broth, following the recipe for smooth woodcock pâté (on page 216) or the pheasant, chestnut and chanterelle soup (on page 197). All the fun of the game bird season is lost if you eat frozen birds through the year, so now is the time to use up odds and ends.

BRAISED MALLARD WITH BLACK PEAS

serves 4

You could make this dish with any of the wild duck family, except perhaps teal, which are quite delicate and better given a brief roasting. Black peas, often called maple peas or carlings, are a bit of a rarity and generally only found up North. If you are struggling to find them, a good alternative would be whole dried green peas.

80g black peas (maple peas or carlings), soaked overnight in cold water

salt and freshly ground black pepper

2 oven-ready mallards

a good knob of butter

1 medium onion, peeled and finely chopped

2 juniper berries, crushed

1 teaspoon thyme leaves

2 teaspoons plain flour

250ml medium cider

350ml hot chicken stock with ½ teaspoon baking powder added

1 tablespoon vegetable oil

Rinse the black peas and put them into a pan of lightly salted fresh water. Bring to the boil and simmer for an hour or so until tender, then drain in a colander.

Halve the mallards lengthways through the backbone and breast and set aside.

Heat the butter in a heavy-based saucepan and gently cook the onion with the juniper and thyme for 2–3 minutes until soft. Stir in the flour and mix well, then gradually add the cider, stirring well to avoid lumps forming. Stir in the chicken stock, season with salt and pepper and bring to the boil. Lower the heat and simmer gently for 30 minutes.

Meanwhile, remove the legs from the mallards and trim around the breasts, removing any excess bones and carcass. Heat the oil in a frying pan. Season both the mallard breasts and legs with salt and pepper. Add to the pan and fry over a medium heat, turning as necessary, for a few minutes until nicely coloured.

Add the legs to the sauce together with the black peas and simmer with the lid on for 40 minutes.

Now add the mallard breasts and simmer for another 10 minutes. By now the sauce should have reduced and thickened slightly; if not remove the legs and breast and set aside, simmer the sauce until reduced to a good consistency, then return the meat. Taste and adjust the seasoning if necessary, then serve.

Combine the two infused liquids in a heavy-based pan. Bring to the boil and boil until reduced by about half. Add the sugar and stir until dissolved, then bring back to the boil and continue to boil for about 5–10 minutes. To test whether the jelly is ready, spoon a little onto a chilled plate and put in the fridge for about 10 minutes; if it sets it is ready. Pour into sterilised jars, seal and store in a cool place or the fridge.

When you are ready to cook the teals, preheat the oven to 230°C/gas 8. Season the birds inside and out and rub with the butter. Roast in the oven for 10–15 minutes, basting once or twice and keeping them nice and pink. Serve with the rosehip jelly on the side.

ROAST TEAL WITH ROSEHIP JELLY
serves 4 as a starter

Tiny teal make a great starter, and the fruity tang of rosehip jelly is the perfect foil. Rosehips can be harvested through the winter and improve after a few frosts as they sweeten up a little. You'll have enough jelly to serve with several other game meals – it keeps well in the fridge.

You could serve the teal with some toast and/or wild salad leaves. For a main course, allow two teal per person.

4 oven-ready teals
salt and freshly ground black pepper
a couple of knobs of softened butter
FOR THE ROSEHIP JELLY
1kg ripe rosehips, stalks removed, washed
3 litres water
1kg sugar

To make the jelly, roughly chop the rosehips. Bring 2 litres water to the boil in a large pan. Add the rosehips, bring back to the boil, then take off the heat and leave to infuse for about 45 minutes. Strain through a jelly bag or a strainer lined with a double layer of muslin into a bowl. Return the pulp to the pan, add the other 1 litre of water and boil for about 15 minutes. Infuse again for 45 minutes then strain through the jelly bag or muslin into a bowl.

GAMEY BROWN WINDSOR SOUP *serves 4–6*

This traditional soup, usually made with beef, is out of favour these days, but like so many old-fashioned dishes that have suffered a dip in popularity, it doesn't deserve its bad reputation and in capable hands can be delicious. I've made it with game here, as I really don't like seeing the carcasses, bones and trimmings going to waste. It's a nourishing, thick wintry affair, especially when boosted with a splash of sherry. I'd recommend taking a flask of soup like this on a shoot or fishing trip.

vegetable oil for frying
150–200g game meat and/or a couple of game carcasses from a roast
1 onion, peeled and roughly chopped
1 small carrot, peeled and roughly chopped
1 small leek, trimmed, roughly chopped and washed
a good knob of butter
2 tablespoons plain flour
1 teaspoon tomato purée
1 garlic clove, peeled and crushed
a few sprigs of thyme
1 small bay leaf
3 litres good beef stock
sea salt and freshly ground black pepper
2 tablespoons cream sherry

Heat the oil in a large heavy-based saucepan and fry the meat and vegetables over a high heat until nicely browned, stirring occasionally. Add the butter, then stir in the flour and cook, stirring, for a couple of minutes. Add the tomato purée, garlic, thyme and bay leaf, then gradually add the beef stock, stirring well to avoid lumps. Bring to the boil and season with salt and pepper. Lower the heat and simmer for 2 hours until the meat is tender.

Pick out a few pieces of meat and set aside. Whiz the rest of the soup to a purée, using a free-standing or hand-held stick blender. Pass through a conical strainer or colander (not a fine sieve) into a pan. The soup should be rich in flavour and a nice brown colour; if not, simmer it a little longer to concentrate the flavour. Add the tender cubes of meat and check the seasoning. Reheat and pour in the sherry just before serving.

GAME FAGGOTS *serves* 4

I've enjoyed the spiced livery flavour of faggots ever since I was a kid. They are good cheap winter fodder, ideal for using up bits and pieces (in this case, game). Generally they're eaten with peas, though at this time of the year I prefer mashed potato, neeps or coarsely mashed parsnips, and/or some creamed Brussels sprouts. To wrap the faggots, you'll need some lamb or pork caul fat, which a butcher should be able to get for you.

I use the mincing attachment of my food mixer to mince the meat, but you could easily use the chopping blade of a food processor.

1 tablespoon vegetable oil

2 small onions, peeled and finely chopped

2 garlic cloves, peeled and crushed

2 teaspoons chopped thyme leaves

3 juniper berries, crushed

200g coarsely minced pork belly

250g coarsely minced pork or game liver

350g coarsely minced game meat (pheasant, wild duck, pigeon, etc.)

100g fresh white breadcrumbs

1 egg, beaten

salt and freshly ground black pepper

½ teaspoon ground mace

200g caul fat (lamb or pig's), soaked for an hour in cold water

FOR THE ONION SAUCE

1 tablespoon vegetable oil

2 medium onions, peeled and thinly sliced

a good knob of butter

3 teaspoons plain flour

1 teaspoon tomato purée

250ml beef stock

Preheat the oven to 220°C/gas 7. Heat the oil in a pan and gently cook the onions and garlic with the thyme and juniper for 2–3 minutes until softened. Add the pork belly and continue cooking for 3–4 minutes, stirring well. Remove from the heat and leave to cool.

Add the liver, game meat, breadcrumbs and egg to the cooled pork mixture and season well with salt, pepper and the mace. Shape the mixture into 150g balls (bigger than a golf ball, but smaller than a tennis ball), then wrap in a double layer of caul fat. Place in a deep baking tray and roast for 20 minutes or so until the faggots are nicely coloured. Drain off the fat.

Meanwhile, make the sauce. Heat the oil in a heavy-based pan, add the onions, cover and cook gently for 8–10 minutes until lightly coloured – you may need to add a splash of water if they start to catch on the bottom of the pan. Add the butter, then the flour and tomato purée and stir well over a low heat for a minute. Gradually add the beef stock, stirring well to avoid lumps forming. Season with salt and pepper, bring to the boil and simmer gently for 20 minutes.

Turn the oven down to 180°C/gas 4. Put the faggots into an ovenproof dish and pour on the sauce. Cover with a lid or foil, and continue cooking for 30 minutes. Serve with seasonal vegetables.

February

Striking red GURNARD *fished from the* Channel, *a veritable feast of* FURRED GAME, *and leafy winter* CABBAGES *for hearty soups, braises and salads...*

OTHER INGREDIENTS NOT TO BE MISSED

Elvers   Pike   Wolf fish   Cod chitterlings   Cuttlefish   Native oysters   Pink prawns

Sprouting broccoli   New season's garlic   Beetroot   Pink Fir Apple potatoes   Bittercress   Chick weed   Sea purslane

Wild watercress   Wild garlic   Wild sorrel   Garlic mustard   Alexanders   Forced rhubarb

February is one of the leaner months for homegrown produce, so we need to be a bit more inventive in the kitchen. We've said goodbye to the game bird season until August, but we do have our year round game – like rabbit, hare, pigeon and venison, all of which make good eating. Hare can, of course, be a bit messy with all that blood and guts, but once cleaned by your butcher or yourself, the meat has the most delicious flavour and texture. Like rabbit, it isn't necessary to slow-cook or braise the whole animal. The saddle gives you tender fillets for flash frying, the legs and shoulders are ideal for braising and pies, and any leftovers can go to make a nice game broth.

The use of the word 'venison' can be a bit misleading as it is the generic term, covering all breeds of deer. But, like buying beef, you need to know what you are eating – whether it is roe deer, red deer, muntjac or fallow deer. With increased farming in recent years, there is plenty of venison of all types to go round – and prices have levelled.

Rather like beef though, many game dealers and butchers still don't get the most out of these beasts. The haunch, for example, tends to get sold in one or two pieces, or diced. But, like a rump of beef, a haunch can be broken down into several muscles, some of which can be as tender as a piece of fillet, while the rest belong in the stewing pot along with the shoulder. The offal is also underused and generally gets thrown away or goes to the hunting dogs … lucky dogs.

As beautiful as they may be, all of these game species are pests and need to be culled on a regular basis, otherwise they disrupt the food chain, causing serious damage to the land, trees and crops. If you live in the countryside or on a farm, you'll probably agree that we should all be eating more furred game – not only because it is great to eat, but also in order to help the environment.

On the subject of the environment, this month I'm featuring gurnard – one of the new third division fish that's making its way up the league table owing to its sustainability. There are three types: the red, the tub (which is pretty similar to the red but larger and rarer), and the grey gurnard, the biggest of the three.

As a kid, I would occasionally land a red gurnard while fishing for other species. When I caught my very first one, I thought I had landed something from the tropics that had swum way off-course! As you take these fish out of the water, their deep red colour and massive protective fin span – designed to ward off predators – are truly impressive.

Their flat armoured faces give them a prehistoric look, rather like pike, but their eating quality is somewhat underrated.

In the past I wouldn't have dreamt of cooking them, nor would the local fishermen – they just ended up as crab and lobster pot bait. Now, though, I'm only too happy to cook these fish, with their lovely meaty flesh.

Cabbages are plentiful now, as indeed they are through the year – from tender spring greens, through summer cabbages, to the robust firm-centred winter cabbages. And they are really not the dull brassicas they make themselves out to be…

One of the best cabbage dishes I have ever tasted was a pointed hispi roasted in a wood-fired oven, served topped with lots of black truffle shavings, at Nobu. So you can see how something as humble as a cabbage can be uplifted beyond its normal status with other good ingredients at hand. Ok, we haven't all got truffles in our fridges and not many of us have wood-fired ovens, but you could team the flavour of a simply roast cabbage with several partners.

Gurnard

Inexpensive and currently sustainable, gurnard are fish we ought to be eating more of. They are one of the most striking of all fish and their meaty white flesh tastes pretty good too. Gurnard lend themselves to all sorts of cooking techniques. They are delicious filleted and coated in a light crisp batter then deep-fried, or just simply pan-fried with sea vegetables. Don't throw the bones away when you fillet them, as they make a great soup (see overleaf).

SOUSED GURNARD WITH SEA PURSLANE
serves 4–6 as a starter or lunch

This is a take on West Country soused mackerel. You can apply various flavourings, but the simpler the better as far as I'm concerned. It makes a great dinner party starter – you could even try sousing two types of fish, such as gurnard and mackerel or red mullet.

2 red gurnard, each about 700g–1kg, scaled, gutted and filleted

2–3 tablespoons cider vinegar

2–3 tablespoons water

1 medium carrot, peeled and thinly sliced

2 medium shallots, peeled and thinly sliced into rings

½ small fennel bulb, thinly sliced

10 coriander seeds

a good pinch of cumin seeds

sea salt

handful of sea purslane, trimmed of any thick stalks and washed

1–2 tablespoons extra virgin rapeseed oil

Preheat the oven to 200°C/gas 6. Check over the gurnard fillets for pin bones, removing any you find with tweezers. Cut larger fillets in half. Lay the gurnard fillets in a shallow dish in which they fit snugly.

Put the cider vinegar, water, carrot, shallots and fennel in a saucepan. Add the spices and 1 teaspoon salt, then bring to the boil. Allow to simmer for a minute, then pour over the fish. Cover with foil and cook in the oven for 10–15 minutes or until the fish is just cooked.

Set aside to cool for a couple of hours. Once cooled, you can refrigerate the dish overnight if preparing ahead, but bring back to room temperature to serve.

When ready to serve, blanch the sea purslane in lightly salted water for a couple of minutes, then drain and refresh under cold water.

Divide the soused gurnard and vegetables among individual serving plates, spooning over the liquor. Scatter over the sea purslane, drizzle lightly with the rapeseed oil and serve.

RED GURNARD SOUP *serves 6–8*

Gurnard are cheap enough to buy just to make a soup, though this is also a great way to use up the bones from either of the other gurnard recipes. I hate throwing fish bones away, so I normally prepare a fish soup or stock straight away, or just freeze the bones if I haven't time to do it there and then. You can use almost any fish bones for this recipe, except oily fish like mackerel and herring.

    1kg red, tub or grey gurnard, scaled and
    gutted
    50ml vegetable oil
    1 large onion, peeled and roughly chopped
    1 leek, trimmed, roughly chopped and
    washed
    1 small fennel bulb, trimmed and roughly
    chopped
    1 red pepper, cored, deseeded and roughly
    chopped
    1 medium potato, peeled and roughly
    chopped
    6 garlic cloves, peeled and chopped
    1 teaspoon fennel seeds
    20 black peppercorns
    2 star anise
    a good pinch of saffron strands
    5 juniper berries
    1 bay leaf
    5g thyme sprigs
    1 tablespoon tomato purée, or to taste
    250g tinned chopped tomatoes
    100ml red wine
    4 litres fish stock
    salt and freshly ground black pepper

Chop the gurnard into pieces, wash and drain well. Heat the oil in a large cooking pot and gently fry the fish, vegetables, garlic, spices, juniper berries and herbs for 10 minutes. Add the tomato purée, chopped tomatoes, red wine and fish stock. Bring to the boil, lower the heat and simmer gently for 50 minutes.

To thicken the soup, ladle about a quarter of it (bones and all) into a blender and whiz until smooth. Return the purée to the pot and simmer for another 15 minutes. The soup should be a rich red colour and have a lightly spiced fish flavour. Add a little more tomato purée if necessary, and season with salt and pepper to taste.

Strain the soup through a sieve or conical strainer and reheat to serve if necessary. Ladle into warm bowls and serve with some good crusty bread.

RED GURNARD WITH SEA SPINACH, STEAMED COCKLES AND BROWN SHRIMPS *serves 4*

Fresh cockles can be as good as any clams, but they do have a tendency to be gritty so before using them, you need to wash them very thoroughly.

    250–300g fresh cockles
    2 red gurnard, each about 800g–1kg,
    scaled and filleted
    2 shallots, peeled and finely chopped
    50ml white wine
    1 tablespoon chopped parsley
    salt and freshly ground black pepper
    100g butter
    60g cooked brown shrimps, peeled
    or whole
    a couple of handfuls of sea spinach,
    trimmed of any thick stalks and
    well washed

To clean the cockles properly, leave them under cold running water for about 15 minutes, agitating them every so often to get rid of any sand. Check over the gurnard fillets for pin bones, removing any you find with tweezers.

Put the shallots in a pan with the white wine and bring to the boil. Add the cockles and parsley, season lightly and cover with a tight-fitting lid. Cook over a high heat for 2–3 minutes, shaking the pan a few times, until the cockles open, then stir in a good knob of butter and the brown shrimps. Discard any cockles that don't open.

While the cockles are steaming, melt 50g of the butter in a non-stick or well-seasoned heavy-based frying pan. Season the gurnard fillets and fry them skin side down over a medium heat for 3 minutes. Lower the heat, turn the fillets and cook for about 2 minutes on the flesh side.

At the same time, blanch the sea spinach in boiling salted water for 2–3 minutes, then drain well. Toss in a pan over a low heat with a generous knob of butter and re-season if necessary.

Pile the sea spinach onto warm plates, lay the gurnard fillets on top and spoon over the cockles, shrimps and cooking liquor to serve.

Venison, rabbit and hare

If you're using young venison or farmed meat, which doesn't have such a strong gamey flavour, marinating it overnight (no longer) in a light marinade of wine, oil, juniper and thyme will improve the flavour. Older animals may benefit from lengthier marinating.

Apart from roasting, game can be used in a variety of interesting ways, including soups, salads, pâtés, pan-fried on toast, etc. The tender inner muscle from a large haunch of venison, roasted rare, makes a great Sunday joint, or you can just cut it into escalopes and flash fry them to eat with seasonal vegetables, or add to a seasonal salad. The rest of the haunch is better slow-cooked in a casserole or for a pie.

Hare has a good gamey flavour. I would always recommend cooking the fillets from the saddle separately, as they are delicious quickly pan-fried and served with vegetables or tossed into a salad. The back and front legs are tough and sinewy – as you'll appreciate if you've ever seen a hare on the move – so they need long slow cooking, in a casserole or pie. Wild rabbits are underutilised game, as they are so abundant in the countryside yet rarely eaten. They are tastier than elusive good free-range chicken and well worth cooking.

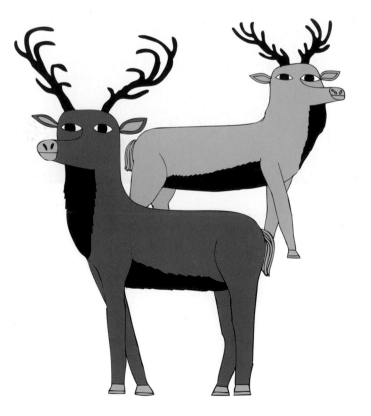

BRAISED VENISON WITH CARROTS *serves 4*

Try to use a singular cut from a seamed haunch, shoulder, neck or shank for this recipe, as the cooking time will then be consistent. If you buy ready-diced meat, it may be a mixture of cuts and there is a risk that some pieces will be tender, while others won't be cooked.

1.5kg trimmed venison meat, from a single muscle

750ml good red wine

2 garlic cloves, peeled and crushed

1 teaspoon thyme leaves, chopped

1 bay leaf

3 juniper berries, crushed

3 tablespoons plain flour

salt and freshly ground black pepper

vegetable oil for frying

60g butter

2 onions, peeled and finely chopped

2 tablespoons tomato purée

1½ litres good dark beef stock

1–2 teaspoons cornflour (optional)

TO SERVE

200–250g small carrots, such as chantenay, peeled

a couple of good knobs of butter

1 teaspoon caster sugar

1 tablespoon chopped parsley

Cut the venison into 3–4cm chunks and place in a stainless steel or ceramic bowl with the red wine, garlic, thyme, bay leaf and juniper berries. Cover and leave to marinate in the fridge for 2 days.

Drain the meat in a colander, reserving the marinade, and dry the pieces on some kitchen paper. Flour the meat lightly, using a tablespoon of the flour, and season with salt and pepper. Heat 2 tablespoons oil in a heavy-based frying pan and fry the meat, a few pieces at a time, over a high heat until nicely browned.

Heat the butter in a large, heavy-based saucepan and gently fry the onions for a few minutes until soft. Add the remaining 2 tablespoons flour and the tomato purée, and stir over a low heat for a minute. Slowly add the reserved marinade, stirring constantly to avoid lumps forming. Bring to the boil and simmer until it has reduced by half.

Add the beef stock and the pieces of venison and bring back to a simmer. Cover with a lid and simmer very gently over a low heat for about 1½ hours until the meat is tender. It's difficult to put an exact time on braising meat; you may find it needs an extra half an hour. Once

the meat is cooked, the sauce should have thickened
sufficiently. If not, mix 1–2 teaspoons cornflour with a
little cold water, stir into the sauce and simmer, stirring,
for a few minutes.

Meanwhile, put the carrots in a pan and just cover with
water. Add the butter, sugar and seasoning and simmer
rapidly until the carrots are tender. Drain off any excess
cooking liquid, leaving a little to glaze them, then toss
with the chopped parsley.

Divide the stew among warm bowls and top with the
glazed carrots. Serve at once.

PEPPERED VENISON CHOPS WITH SWEET AND SOUR RED ONIONS *serves* 4

Chops are a nice, easy way to cook venison. Perhaps surprisingly, since it's a pretty economical way to prepare a large saddle, chops are not a standard venison cut, so you may well need to order some from your butcher or game dealer.

    4 large red onions
    a couple of good knobs of butter
    1 tablespoon malt vinegar
    1 tablespoon redcurrant jelly
    salt and freshly ground black pepper
    8 venison chops, each about 120–150g
    vegetable oil for brushing

Preheat the oven to 200°C/gas 6. Place the whole red onions on a baking tray and bake for about an hour or so, or until soft. Leave to cool for a while, then remove the skins, quarter the onions and separate into 'petals'.

Melt the butter in a frying pan over a low heat, add the onions, vinegar and redcurrant jelly, season with salt and pepper and cook gently for 4–5 minutes or so until the liquid has evaporated and the onions are nice and glossy.

Meanwhile, heat a ridged griddle or heavy-based frying pan. Season the chops with salt and liberally with coarsely ground black pepper. Brush the griddle pan with a little oil and cook the chops for 4–5 minutes on each side, keeping them nice and pink.

Spoon the red onions onto warm serving plates and place the venison chops on top. Serve at once.

SADDLE OF HARE WITH BEETROOT MASH *serves* 4

You should be able to get two decent portions from a saddle once filleted, saving the rest of the hare for a casserole or pie. I've used two types of beetroot here: the common red beetroot, finely shredded and gently cooked with red onions and a touch of cider vinegar; and the white or yellow beetroot, cooked and mashed for the surprise element.

    the saddle fillets from 2 large hares
    a couple of good knobs of butter
    1 large red onion, peeled and chopped
    150–170g red beetroot, peeled and finely
    chopped or shredded
    1 teaspoon thyme leaves
    1 tablespoon cider vinegar
    1 teaspoon redcurrant jelly
    150ml chicken stock
    salt and freshly ground black pepper
    1–2 tablespoons vegetable or corn oil
    FOR THE PALE BEETROOT MASH
    300g yellow or white beetroot, peeled and
    quartered
    a couple of good knobs of butter

For the beetroot mash, cook the beetroot in simmering, salted water for about 40 minutes or until very tender.

Set the hare fillets aside to bring to room temperature. Heat a knob of butter in a saucepan and add the onion, red beetroot and thyme. Cover and cook over a very low heat for about 30 minutes, stirring occasionally and adding a splash of water if the pan is getting dry.

When the beetroot for the mash are cooked, drain and coarsely mash with a potato masher. Return to the pan, mix in the butter and season to taste; keep warm.

Add the cider vinegar and redcurrant jelly to the red beetroot, season and cook for another 5 minutes or so without the lid on, stirring every so often. Add the chicken stock and continue simmering until there are just 2 or 3 spoonfuls of liquor left in the pan; keep warm.

Season the hare fillets with salt and pepper. Heat the oil in a frying pan and cook the fillets for 3–5 minutes over a fairly high heat, turning them every so often and keeping them quite rare. The thickness of the fillets will determine the cooking time, but it's important not to overcook them.

To serve, spoon the red onion and beetroot mixture onto warm serving plates with the cooking liquor. Cut each hare fillet into 3 or 4 slices and arrange on top. Spoon the pale beetroot mash alongside and serve.

RABBIT BRAWN *serves 6–8*

This is a perfect dish for using the front and back legs and the carcass of a rabbit if you've just used the fillets, say for a salad. Piccalilli (see page 15) makes a great accompaniment, or you can simple slice the brawn thinly to cover a plate for a starter, or serve it on hot toast.

- 1 pig's trotter, chopped or sawn into 4–5 pieces
- 1 onion, peeled and halved
- 2 garlic cloves, peeled
- 2 teaspoons sea salt
- the carcass and back and front legs from 2 rabbits

FOR THE BOUQUET GARNI
- 1 bay leaf
- a sprig of thyme
- 12 coriander seeds
- 12 white peppercorns

For the bouquet garni, tie the herbs and spices in a square of muslin to make a bag, securing with string. Put into a large saucepan with the pig's trotter, onion, garlic and salt. Pour in enough water to cover the trotter, then bring to a simmer. Skim off the scum from the surface and simmer for 1 hour, skimming every so often.

Add the rabbit to the pan and continue to simmer and skim for a further hour. By this time, the rabbit meat should be coming off the bone and the pig's trotter disintegrating. If not, continue simmering for another half an hour or so.

Tip into a colander over a bowl to save the liquor, then strain the liquid through a fine sieve back into the cleaned pan. Return to the heat and boil until it has reduced to a sticky liquid, about 200ml in volume. Taste and adjust the seasoning if necessary. Leave to cool, but not until set.

Remove all of the meat from the rabbit and pig's trotter, including all the bits of gelatinous skin. Mix the pieces of meat with the liquid and transfer to a terrine mould, bowl, pie dish or other suitable container. Cover with cling film and place in the fridge. Leave to set overnight.

To serve, cut the rabbit brawn into very fine slices using a very sharp knife and arrange over individual plates. Alternatively, cut into thicker slices and serve with hot toast and a leafy salad.

GAMEKEEPER'S PIE *serves 4–6*

This is a gamey version of a Shepherd's pie, with parsnip added to the mash topping to give it that savoury and sweet flavour. You can just use the meat from the shoulder or tougher haunch cuts of venison, or a mixture of, say, hare and venison with some rabbit thrown in.

1kg coarsely minced venison, or a mixture of game

salt and freshly ground black pepper

3–4 tablespoons vegetable oil

3 medium onions, peeled and finely chopped

2 garlic cloves, peeled and crushed

4 juniper berries, crushed

1 teaspoon chopped thyme leaves

1 tablespoon plain flour

1 tablespoon tomato purée

1 tablespoon Worcestershire sauce

200ml cider

1 litre good beef stock

FOR THE MASH TOPPING

2–3 large potatoes (recommended for mash), peeled and quartered

200g parsnips, peeled, cored and roughly chopped

a few good knobs of butter

splash of milk (optional)

Season the minced venison or other game with salt and pepper. Heat 1–2 tablespoons oil in a heavy-based frying pan until it is almost smoking, then brown the meat in small batches for a few minutes, turning it with a wooden spoon. Drain in a colander to remove all the fat.

Heat 2 tablespoons oil in a heavy-based saucepan and gently fry the onions with the garlic, juniper and chopped thyme until very soft. Add the meat, dust it with the flour and add the tomato purée. Cook for a few minutes, stirring constantly.

Add the Worcestershire sauce, then slowly stir in the cider and beef stock. Bring to a simmer and cook gently for about 1 hour until the liquid has thickened. Check the seasoning and set aside to cool. Preheat the oven to 200°C/gas 6.

Meanwhile, for the mash, cook the potatoes and parsnips separately in boiling salted water for about 10–12 minutes until soft. Drain in a colander, then return to their pans on a low heat for a minute or so to evaporate any excess water. Mash the potatoes and parsnips together smoothly with a potato masher, adding the butter and a little milk if necessary. Season with salt and pepper to taste.

Spoon the meat mixture into a large pie dish or individual dishes and spoon the mash evenly on top. Rough up the surface with a fork and bake for 35–40 minutes until the topping is golden.

Cabbage

Cabbages of all types are brilliant at taking other flavours on board. One of the most common pairings is with smoky bacon and onions, which makes a good side dish for game, duck, poultry and red meats. I've even served it with fish, sometimes replacing the bacon with off-cuts of smoked salmon as a non-meaty alternative. And cabbage on its own is actually a great accompaniment to fish like salmon, pollack and haddock.

Do make the most of all the different varieties of cabbage as they come into season throughout the year. Apart from serving them as an accompaniment, they are also excellent in wintry soups, and finely shredded in salads.

CABBAGE AND BACON SOUP *serves 4–6*

A hearty soup to keep the winter chill out. Cabbage and bacon – especially smoked bacon – are the perfect partners. Try to buy a whole piece of smoked streaky bacon, so that you can cut it into good-sized pieces for a chunky soup.

150–200g piece of smoked streaky bacon

a good knob of butter

1 large onion, peeled and finely chopped

2 garlic cloves, peeled and crushed

2 litres good chicken stock

salt and freshly ground black pepper

8–10 leaves of Savoy, pointed hispi or green cabbage

10–12 small waxy potatoes, such as Anya, Ratte or Charlotte, peeled

2 tablespoons coarsely chopped parsley

Cut the bacon roughly into 1cm cubes. Heat the butter in a large saucepan and add the onion, garlic and bacon. Cover the pan and cook gently for 4–5 minutes, stirring every so often. Add the stock, bring to the boil and simmer gently for 40 minutes.

Meanwhile, cut the cabbage leaves roughly into 1cm pieces and thinly slice the potatoes. Add the cabbage and potatoes to the pan with a little salt and some pepper and simmer for 10–12 minutes.

Add the chopped parsley and check the seasoning. Simmer for another couple of minutes.

Ladle the soup into warm bowls and serve with some good bread.

WINTER COLESLAW *serves 6–8*

Cabbage and carrots are the classic coleslaw components, but by adding some shredded kohlrabi or turnip, and maybe some red cabbage, you can take this rudimentary salad to a whole new level. Beyond hamburgers and crumbed chicken drumsticks, coleslaw goes with various other foods, including hot smoked mackerel or salmon.

½ small head of red cabbage, trimmed

½ small head of white cabbage, trimmed

2 large carrots, trimmed and peeled

½ small head of celeriac, peeled

1 medium kohlrabi or turnip, peeled

1 medium red onion, peeled, halved and finely sliced

salt and freshly ground black pepper

5–6 tablespoons good quality mayonnaise (see page 119)

Slice the red and white cabbage halves in two and cut out the core. Shred the leaves as finely as possible, using a sharp chopping knife. Slice the carrots, celeriac and kohlrabi into thin matchsticks, by cutting them into 3–4cm lengths with a sharp knife, then into thin slices, then into sticks. (Alternatively, use a mandolin.)

In a large bowl, mix the cabbage with the onion and root vegetable matchsticks. Season with salt and pepper, add the mayonnaise and toss to mix. Leave to stand for about 20 minutes. Before serving, give the coleslaw a final mix and check the seasoning.

FRIED DUCK'S EGG WITH SAVOY CABBAGE AND SMOKED SALMON *serves 4*

The combination of smoked salmon and cabbage works rather like cabbage and bacon – you only need a small amount of smoked salmon or the flavour takes over. Use smoked salmon trimmings, or even trimmings from hot smoked salmon – Braden rost (see page 143).

1 small head of Savoy cabbage, trimmed

salt and freshly ground black pepper

a couple of good knobs of butter

1 medium onion, peeled, halved and finely sliced

60g smoked salmon, or trimmings, chopped

2–3 tablespoons rapeseed or vegetable oil

4 duck's eggs

Quarter, core and finely shred the cabbage. Bring a pan of salted water to the boil and blanch the cabbage for 2–3 minutes, then drain well.

Meanwhile, heat the butter in a large pan and gently cook the onion for 3–4 minutes, stirring every so often, until soft. Add the cabbage and season with salt and pepper. Cover the pan and cook over a low heat for about 8–10 minutes, stirring every so often, until the cabbage is tender. Stir in the smoked salmon, re-season if necessary and keep warm.

Meanwhile, heat the rapeseed oil in a large frying pan and fry the duck's eggs for 3–4 minutes or until cooked to your liking. Spoon the cabbage onto warm plates and top each serving with a fried egg. Serve at once.

BACON CHOP WITH RED CABBAGE AND PRUNES *serves 4*

I tried this out at home one night after I had been on an experimental bacon curing session. Red cabbage and raisins is a classic pairing, so I thought why not try it with prunes as they have something of an affiliation with bacon in classic French cooking. It worked a treat!

Home-cured bacon chops would be ideal here, but otherwise ask your butcher if he can lay his hands on a piece of smoked streaky or back bacon with the bone in. Thick pieces of bacon like this can tend to be a bit on the salty side, so I recommend blanching them first.

4 bacon chops, each about 180–200g (see above)

a couple of good knobs of butter

1 large red onion, peeled, halved and thinly sliced

1 small head of red cabbage, quartered, root removed and very finely shredded

salt and freshly ground black pepper

1 teaspoon redcurrant jelly

8 no-need-to-soak prunes, pitted and shredded

vegetable oil for frying

Add the bacon chops to a pan of cold water, bring to the boil and blanch for 6–7 minutes, then drain.

Heat the butter in a large saucepan, add the red onion and cook gently for 3–4 minutes until soft. Add the cabbage, season with salt and pepper and cover with the lid. Cook over a very low heat for 10 minutes, stirring every so often. Add the redcurrant jelly and prunes and

continue to cook, covered, for a further 10–15 minutes, stirring every so often, until the cabbage is soft. Taste and adjust the seasoning if necessary and keep warm.

Heat a little oil in a large heavy-based frying pan and fry the bacon chops for about 4–5 minutes on each side until golden brown and tender. Remove and drain on kitchen paper.

Spoon the red cabbage and prunes onto warm serving plates and place a bacon chop alongside. Serve at once.

March

Subtle WILD GARLIC *leaves gathered from riverbanks and* damp, shady woods *and beautiful* PURPLE-SPROUTING BROCCOLI – *the first of the tender spring vegetables...*

OTHER INGREDIENTS NOT TO BE MISSED

Wild salmon   Sea trout   Wild char   Elvers   Sprats   Razor clams   Spring lamb   Guinea fowl eggs

Pheasant eggs   Beetroot   New season's garlic   Pennywort   Sea beet   Bittercress   Wood sorrel   Wild chervil

Water celery   Watercress   Alexanders   Dittander

March isn't the most prolific month for seasonal produce, as we are somewhat in between seasons for vegetables and fruit, especially. Of course there are still plenty of good winter cabbages, cauliflowers and roots around, but one not-to-be-missed vegetable that shows up around this time of the year is purple-sprouting broccoli. The king of broccoli, it is, in my view, one of the most underrated vegetables. For me, it is in the asparagus league – or at least it should be – and it can be served in a similar way. It has an evocative look about it, like asparagus – inviting you to pick up the spears with your fingers and dunk them in melted butter or silky hollandaise.

You do, however, need to be choosy when buying this vegetable. Sprouting broccoli can vary enormously, as some farmers don't look after the crop in the way that they should. When I visited British producer Peter Ashcroft in Lancashire he taught me the techniques of careful nurturing. It might be time-consuming, but cutting new flowering stems on a regular basis encourages more sprouts to form, which not only gives a better yield of slim, tender stalks, it also prolongs the season. You often come across sprouting broccoli with thick, woody stalks, which hasn't been looked after properly and can be virtually inedible.

Look for slender, almost scrawny stems and leaves with a good colour that are reasonably firm. By the way, this vegetable is nothing like its dull cousins, broccoli and calabrese, which I regard more as a convenience vegetable, like peas. I'm always disappointed when the purple-sprouting broccoli season draws to a close, but at least it makes another appearance – towards the end of autumn.

At this time of year, you may well have noticed a waft of garlic while walking through the woods or driving in the country with your window down and wondered where on earth the smell is coming from. Wild garlic grows prolifically in dark, damp woods and once you recognise the green leafy herb, like me, you won't be able to resist picking it. It's got a lovely mild garlicky flavour and has a multitude of uses. I find it is delicious in soups and sauces, and you can even throw the leaves into robust salads.

I lifted some wild garlic with the roots while foraging a few years back and planted it in an old tub along with parsley, so I now have my own small supply. You could easily do the same. It is probably better contained in a tub as otherwise it would most likely take over the garden. You just need to make sure it is in the shade and give it plenty of water. When the wild garlic dies off, the parsley takes its place and vice versa.

Hedgerow garlic, sometimes called three-cornered garlic, is another member of the family that can be used in much the same way as wild garlic leaves. It's often found along footpaths and could be easily mistaken for thick blades of grass. In appearance, it is similar to garlic chives. Its snowbell-like white flowers give it the alternative name of snowbell garlic.

I'm usually looking forward to getting a bit of early salmon fishing in around the end of this month, though the fish are a bit few and far between. I'll often end up catching kelt fish that have spawned and are on their way back. An early fresh fish on his way up the river is always a bit of a bonus, especially if you've been avoiding farmed salmon for the last few months.

Wild garlic

Of all the wild herbs that are up for grabs for free, wild garlic must be the most versatile. Along with the other kinds of garlic, it appears abundantly on my menus at this time of year. Almost as adaptable as parsley, it can be chopped and used as a flavouring, blended to make a soup or sauce, or served more like a vegetable. I often blitz some with olive oil – like a pesto – to keep in the fridge for tossing into sauces, dressings and pasta dishes. Even the flowers can be deep-fried in a light batter in the same way as courgette flowers, at the end of the season in a couple of months.

WILD GARLIC AND NETTLE SOUP *serves 4*

When you have great wild ingredients at hand, it makes sense to use them. Both young nettles and wild garlic are abundant at this time of year and easy to gather – just remember to take a rubber glove with you for gathering the nettles. And don't worry, cooking takes the prickle out of young nettles so they aren't going to sting your throat on the way down.

    a couple of good knobs of butter
    2 leeks, trimmed, chopped and washed
    1 tablespoon plain flour
    1.5 litres hot vegetable stock
    salt and freshly ground black pepper
    handful of young nettle tops
    handful of wild garlic leaves, washed and
      chopped
    3–4 tablespoons double cream

Melt the butter in a heavy-based pan and gently cook the leeks for 2–3 minutes to soften, stirring every so often. Stir in the flour, then gradually stir in the hot vegetable stock and season with salt and pepper. Bring to the boil, lower the heat and simmer for about 20 minutes.

Add about two-thirds of the nettles and wild garlic leaves and simmer for a few minutes. Whiz the soup in a blender until smooth, in batches if necessary, then return to the pan.

Stir in the cream and the rest of the nettles and wild garlic. Simmer for a few more minutes, then taste and adjust the seasoning if necessary. Serve piping hot, with some good bread.

RAZOR CLAMS WITH WILD BOAR BACON AND HEDGEROW GARLIC *serves 4 as a starter*

Razor clams are the oddest of shellfish and not commonly found in fishmongers. They have a texture and flavour somewhere between scallops and squid and, like these shellfish, they'll turn rubbery if you overcook them.

    8 or 12 live razor clams
    150g wild boar bacon or normal bacon,
      in one piece
    ½ glass white wine
    a few sprigs of thyme
    a few parsley stalks
    3 garlic cloves, peeled and roughly
      chopped
    1 teaspoon salt
    1 tablespoon vegetable oil
    50g butter
    handful of hedgerow garlic, chopped

Preheat the oven to 150°C/gas 2. Wash the razor clams under cold running water for 10 minutes. Meanwhile, chop the bacon roughly into 1cm pieces, blanch in boiling water for 2 minutes, then drain and set aside.

Put the razor clams into a cooking pot with the white wine, thyme, parsley stalks, garlic and salt. Cover with a tight-fitting lid and cook over a high heat for a couple of minutes, giving the occasional stir, until the shells are just starting to open. Drain in a colander.

When cool enough to handle, carefully remove the clams from their shells, keeping the shells intact. Cut away the dark looking sac and discard, then cut each clam into two or three pieces. Lay the razor shells in a warm shallow baking dish.

Heat the oil in a pan and fry the bacon over a medium heat for a couple minutes until lightly coloured. Add the butter and hedgerow garlic.

Arrange the clams in their shells, scattering over the bacon and garlic mixture. Warm through in the oven for a couple of minutes, then serve.

BRAISED CUTTLEFISH WITH WILD GARLIC *serves 4 as a starter*

Cuttlefish is so underused in the UK. Our fishermen land tons of the stuff, yet we seem to be quite content eating frozen squid. It really doesn't make sense. Cuttlefish can be used in exactly the same way as squid; you can even deep-fry them coated in batter or breadcrumbs if you like.

If you buy cuttlefish uncleaned, it should have a certain amount of ink in its body pouch, which you can save, although it can sometimes be gritty. Alternatively, you can buy squid and cuttlefish ink separately from fishmongers – in handy little pouches that you can keep in the freezer ready for whenever you need them. Here you would need 3–4 sachets if your cuttlefish has already shed its ink.

1kg cuttlefish, cleaned and ink reserved

salt and freshly ground black pepper

1 tablespoon vegetable oil

a couple of good knobs of butter

2 shallots, peeled, halved and finely chopped

2 garlic cloves, peeled and crushed

1 tablespoon plain flour

100ml white wine

250ml hot fish stock

reserved cuttlefish ink (or 3–4 sachets)

handful of wild garlic leaves

Wash the cuttlefish in cold water, then pat dry with some kitchen paper. Cut roughly into 3cm pieces and season with salt and pepper.

Heat the oil in a heavy-based frying pan and fry the cuttlefish pieces over a high heat for a few minutes until golden, then drain and set aside.

Melt the butter in a clean pan and cook the shallots and garlic for 2–3 minutes until softened, then stir in the flour. Now gradually add the white wine and fish stock, stirring well to avoid lumps forming as you do so. Bring to the boil, season and add the cuttlefish and ink.

Simmer gently for about 30–40 minutes or until the cuttlefish is tender, then stir in the wild garlic leaves and simmer for a couple more minutes before serving.

ROAST FREE-RANGE CHICKEN WITH WILD GARLIC SAUCE *serves 4*

This garlic sauce is a variation on bread sauce and is a great match for simple roast chicken. Out of the wild garlic season, you can make it just with the baked garlic or if you've preserved some pesto-fashion (see page 46), you can just stir in a couple of spoonfuls or so at the end. I think gravy often drowns the natural flavours of a good chicken, whereas a sauce like this acts more like a dip.

1 free-range chicken, about 1.5kg

salt and freshly ground black pepper

a few sprigs of thyme

a few sprigs of rosemary

80–100g duck or goose fat

a little oil for the tray

FOR THE WILD GARLIC SAUCE

1 head of new season's garlic

3–4 tablespoons water

60–70g fresh white breadcrumbs

handful or two of wild garlic leaves, washed and dried

Preheat the oven to 200°C/gas 6. Season the chicken inside and out. Pop the thyme and rosemary sprigs into its cavity, along with the whole garlic bulb for the sauce, and rub the duck fat over the breasts and legs. Place in a lightly oiled roasting tray, resting the bird on one leg, rather than placing it upright.

Roast the chicken in the oven, basting regularly. After 25 minutes, turn it onto the other leg. Roast for another 25 minutes, then finish cooking breast uppermost. Test the chicken after 1¼ hours: the juices should run clear when a skewer or knife tip is inserted into the thickest part of the thigh. When cooked, transfer the chicken to a warm platter and rest in a warm place for 15 minutes, reserving the juices and fat in the roasting tray.

While the chicken is resting, make the sauce: remove the garlic from the bird then halve it and squeeze or scoop out the soft inner flesh. Warm the fat in the roasting tray with the water, scraping up the sediment from the bottom of the tray. Put the breadcrumbs and garlic flesh in a blender with the liquor from the roasting tray and whiz briefly, then transfer to a saucepan and season with salt and pepper to taste. Roughly chop the wild garlic leaves and stir into the sauce. Simmer gently for a few minutes, then transfer to a warm sauceboat.

Serve the chicken, carved or jointed with the garlic sauce and purple-sprouting broccoli or other vegetables.

SCALLOPS WITH PURPLE-SPROUTING BROCCOLI *serves 4 as a starter*

Sprouting broccoli isn't often paired with such posh partners, but it is a perfect foil for firm, sweet scallops and makes a great seasonal starter. Ideally buy scallops in the shell and prepare them yourself, or at least buy them freshly shucked. I now keep the muscle on scallops, as it seems such a waste to trim it off. Likewise I don't discard the corals. Here I've sautéed them until they start to crisp up to give them an appetising texture.

8 small tender stems of purple-sprouting broccoli

salt and freshly ground black pepper

100g butter

12 medium scallops, shelled and cleaned

Trim the nice purple heads and a few leaves from the sprouting broccoli and put to one side. Chop the rest and cook in a pan of boiling salted water for 4–5 minutes until tender, then drain and whiz in a blender or food processor until smooth. Transfer to a clean pan, season with salt and pepper to taste and add a couple of knobs of the butter; keep warm.

Remove the corals from the scallops and cut in half if large. Heat about a third of the remaining butter in a heavy-based frying pan. Season the corals and fry for 4–5 minutes, turning them every so often until crisp.

Meanwhile, add the purple heads and leaves to a pan of boiling salted water and cook for about 3 minutes until tender, then drain.

When the corals are crisp, remove and set aside. Wipe out the pan, then rub some of the remaining butter over the base and place over a medium-high heat. Season the scallops and cook for just 1 minute on each side, then add the rest of the butter, the fried corals and the broccoli heads and leaves.

Spoon the broccoli purée onto warm plates, arrange the scallops, corals and broccoli on top and serve at once.

Purple-sprouting broccoli

Purple-sprouting broccoli is so much more versatile than ordinary broccoli, which is far too common both in and out of its natural season for my liking. Of course you can serve purple-sprouting as a vegetable in the same way, but in addition, you'll find it is delicious served with hollandaise, or drizzled with olive oil and topped with shavings of pecorino or Parmesan, or simply tossed in melted butter – as you might asparagus. Sprouting broccoli makes a great fresh-tasting puréed soup. It's also perfect for dipping into a classic cheese fondue, as the flowery heads retain the sauce well.

PURPLE-SPROUTING BROCCOLI WITH PICKLED WALNUTS AND ROASTED GARLIC *serves* 4

Be sure to buy slender, young stems of broccoli as thicker stalks tend to be woody. Also be aware that there are fakes on the market trying to pass themselves off as purple-sprouting, which won't taste like the real thing.

1 head of new season's garlic

4–5 pickled walnuts

700–800g tender purple-sprouting broccoli stems

salt and freshly ground black pepper

a couple of good knobs of butter

Preheat the oven to 200°C/gas 6. Wrap the garlic in foil and bake for 45 minutes, then unwrap and leave until cool enough to handle. Separate the cloves of garlic and remove the skin. Cut each of the pickled walnuts into 3 or 4 pieces.

Add the broccoli to a pan of boiling salted water and cook for 3–4 minutes or until tender. Meanwhile, heat the butter in a pan with the garlic and some seasoning.

Drain the broccoli as soon as it is ready. Transfer to a warm serving dish and spoon over the garlicky butter. Scatter the pickled walnuts over the broccoli and serve.

PURPLE-SPROUTING BROCCOLI TART WITH BEENLEIGH BLUE *serves* 4

This tart makes a good starter or light lunch, served with a salad – you could even take it on a picnic. Here I've used Beenleigh blue, a cheese from the Southwest, but you could use goat's cheese or even shave a mature Lancashire over the tart when it comes out of the oven, as you would Parmesan.

500g ready-made butter puff pastry

1 egg, beaten

700–800g small tender stems of purple-sprouting broccoli

salt and freshly ground black pepper

30g grated mature Cheddar

50g butter

60–80g Beenleigh blue

Roll out the pastry to a 3mm thickness and cut 4 rectangles, each about 14 x 11cm. Prick them all over with a fork, then place them on a large baking tray. Cut 1cm wide strips from the rest of the pastry, as long as you can. Brush the edges of the rectangles with beaten egg. Lay the strips along all four sides and trim to form a neat raised border. Crimp these edges with a pastry crimper, or press half-moons along them with the blade of a knife. Brush the edges with beaten egg. Leave to rest in the fridge for 1 hour.

Trim the top 10cm of the sprouting broccoli stems, saving the rest for the purée. Bring two pans of salted water to the boil. Cook the broccoli tips and leaves for 3–4 minutes until tender, then drain and refresh in cold water to stop them discolouring; drain well and set aside.

Cook the trimmings in the other pan for 4–5 minutes or until soft, then drain and tip into a blender or food processor. Add the grated Cheddar, butter and some salt and pepper, then whiz to a coarse purée. Taste and adjust the seasoning.

Preheat the oven to 160°C/gas 3. Cut 4 rectangles of cardboard to fit just inside the pastry edges and wrap in a double layer of foil. Place one in each pastry case to cover the centre. Bake for 8–10 minutes, then remove from the oven and lift out the foil-wrapped cardboard. Turn the oven up to 200°C/gas 6.

Spread about a tablespoon of the broccoli purée in the middle of each tart. Don't put too much in; save what's left for a dip or sauce. Lay the blanched broccoli, as close together as you can, over the purée and season with salt and pepper. Lay some buttered foil loosely on top, to cover the broccoli but not the pastry edges. Bake the tarts for about 10 minutes, then remove the foil and crumble the Beenleigh blue over the broccoli. Serve immediately.

April

Leafy CELERY *from the* Fenlands, ST GEORGE'S MUSHROOMS *foraged from woodlands and* OUTDOOR RHUBARB *– the first native fruit of the year...*

OTHER INGREDIENTS NOT TO BE MISSED

Wild salmon   Sea trout   Elvers   Herring   Spring lamb   Gull's eggs   Pheasant eggs

Spring greens   Purple-sprouting broccoli   Cornish early asparagus   Jersey royals   Cornish early potatoes

Wild garlic   Hogweed   Wild radish leaves   Nettles   Bristly ox tongue   Sea purslane   Wild radish leaf   Morels

April brings us a bit closer to spring as we know it. The season might officially start in March, but from a culinary perspective it arrives much later. Even in April it's just not quite warm enough for most spring veg. Instead we are relying on purple-sprouting broccoli, the last of the winter crops and good all-rounders, like celery.

Traditionally white English Fenland celery is in season from October through to January. During the winter, soil would be piled up around the stems to protect them from the cold and blanch them at the same time. Over the years, new varieties of celery have been introduced so both green and white varieties can be harvested virtually all the year round.

Celery is a versatile vegetable that's underused in my opinion. Most people think of it as something you just cram into a tumbler to serve with cheese, but it makes a great soup, adds flavour to stews and casseroles, and is delicious served in salads or braised as an accompaniment. A large head of leafy English celery can go a long way. Unfortunately it's usually sold trimmed so that it fits into those

convenient plastic sleeves. Look out for the more inviting leafy heads in farmers' markets and good greengrocers. You'll get more out of them, including plenty of leaves to use in a salad or to make a pot of celery salt (see page 58).

Our first really serious fungi, the St George's mushroom shows up this month. The name hardly warrants explanation... even if you don't follow the religious calendar. In theory, the mushroom makes its first appearance of the year around St George's day (23ʳᵈ April), but in reality it is often more abundant from around the end of the month through to mid-May. In France the St George's is revered as a prize mushroom, but here only staunch foragers give it due respect.

St George's mushrooms are pretty tricky to detect, so I'd advise you to go with a pro if you haven't foraged for them before. Rather like cupped field mushrooms, without the black spores and with a much firmer texture, they do vary in size considerably. Larger ones are a little stronger on the nose and rather mealy-like, but that flavour dissipates during cooking. They grow in rings, which should make them easy to spot, but whenever I've been foraging for them, they've always been well hidden under heavily matted grass.

It's rare to find St George's mushrooms in greengrocers or markets, so you need to be a resolute mushroom gatherer to find them, or know someone who is. Foraging is certainly a weekend pursuit I'd recommend – fresh air, exercise and great food for free.

Unless you're a gardener, you may be confused by the rhubarb season. From late December through to March, forced rhubarb from the famous Yorkshire 'Rhubarb Triangle' is in the shops, but now it's time for outdoor rhubarb. This is certainly much more robust and flavoursome, although it hasn't got the delicate appearance of the indoor grown stuff.

Towards the end of this month, weather permitting, we also welcome the first British asparagus from St Enedoc in Cornwall where the favourable microclimate gives everything a little head start. Cornish new potatoes are also a bit of a treat at this time of the year to rival Jersey Royals and give a real sense that spring is close.

Celery

From soups to salads, there are plenty of ways to use celery and I reckon it's only a matter of time before this vegetable makes its way back onto menus. To get the most out of celery, as I've said, you do need to seek out leafy heads, as the leaves have as much to offer as the stalks in my view. Of course the stalks add flavour to all kinds of soups, stews and other cooked dishes, and they are delicious pickled in cider vinegar to serve as an accompaniment to pâtés, cold meat and fish.

The leaves are great in salads and you can also use them to make your own celery salt, which is far superior to any you can buy. Simply chop the leaves from a head of celery, scatter them on a large baking tray and dry in the oven on its lowest setting for around 8 hours until crisp (don't let them brown). Once dry, whiz in a blender with a handful of sea salt flakes to a powder. Store in a screw-topped jar.

CELERY AND STILTON SOUP *serves 4–6*

Celery and Stilton are familiar cheeseboard partners, but they also marry brilliantly in a soup. Serve this with some good, crusty bread.

1 small leafy head of celery
a good knob of butter
1 small onion, peeled and chopped
1½ litres vegetable stock
salt and freshly ground black pepper
2 tablespoons double cream
60g Stilton, rind removed, cut into chunks
1 teaspoon celery salt (see above)

Separate the leaves from the celery stalks, wash and pat dry, then set the leaves aside. Roughly chop the stalks.

Heat the butter in a medium saucepan. Add the onion and celery, cover and cook gently for 3–4 minutes to soften, stirring occasionally. Add the stock, season lightly and bring to a simmer. Cover and simmer for 30 minutes. Now add all but a handful of the celery leaves and simmer for another 5–6 minutes. Remove from the heat.

Whiz the soup to a purée in a blender, in batches if necessary. Pass through a sieve into a clean pan to remove any stringy bits. Reheat if necessary and stir in the cream.

Pour into warm soup plates and crumble in the Stilton. Roughly tear the reserved celery leaves and scatter over the soup. Sprinkle with a little celery salt and serve.

BRAISED CELERY HEARTS *serves 4*

These can be served as an accompaniment to most meat and fish dishes, or even as a part of a buffet. Don't discard the outer stalks – use them to make a soup or flavour a casserole.

2 celery heads (with leaves)
salt and freshly ground black pepper
about 500ml hot vegetable stock
300ml double cream

Preheat the oven to 190°C/gas 5. Remove the outer stalks from the celery and save the leaves for the sauce.

Put the celery hearts into an ovenproof dish, season with salt and pepper and pour over the vegetable stock. Cover with a lid or foil and cook for 1 hour or until the celery hearts are tender when tested with the point of a knife. Drain in a colander, reserving the stock, then halve or quarter the celery hearts and set aside.

Put about half of the reserved stock into a saucepan and boil until it has reduced to just a few tablespoons. Add the cream, bring to the boil and simmer until the sauce has reduced by about half and thickened.

Chop the celery leaves very finely and add them to the sauce. Taste and adjust the seasoning and simmer for a couple of minutes. Add the celery hearts and warm through briefly, then serve.

CELERY AND PICKLED WALNUT SALAD
serves 4

This makes a nice refreshing starter or side side, or you could serve it with a cheese course. For a more substantial starter, crumble in some blue cheese or goat's cheese. I never quite seem to get the timing right to capture walnuts at their perfect soft shell stage for pickling, so I've usually had to rely on shop-bought ones. Luckily Jason Lowe had pickled a few jars last autumn, which inspired me to concoct this simple salad while we were photographing the book.

1 head of very leafy celery (you may need 2 heads to obtain enough leaves)

12 pickled walnuts (or more)

FOR THE DRESSING

1 teaspoon walnut pickling vinegar

1 tablespoon cider vinegar

3–4 tablespoons extra virgin rapeseed oil

1 teaspoon English mustard, such as Tewksbury or grainy Norfolk mustard

salt and freshly ground black pepper

Remove all the leaves from the celery and give them a good wash and dry. Tear larger leaves into smaller pieces. Finely slice the celery hearts and place them in a bowl with the leaves. (Use the rest of the celery stalks to flavour a soup or casserole.)

To make the dressing, whisk all of the ingredients together in a bowl to combine, seasoning with salt and pepper to taste.

Drizzle the dressing over the celery and toss lightly. Arrange on individual plates. Scatter the walnuts over the salad, breaking any large ones in half. Serve at once.

St George's mushrooms

It is terrific to have a real British wild mushroom to work with at this time of the year. Mainstream mushrooms – chanterelles, ceps, girolles, hedgehog fungus and alike – are autumnal so the St George's mushroom is deservedly a celebrated fungi. It can be used in much the same way as most wild mushrooms. It has a great meaty texture, so it's well suited to braised dishes. St George's is also a great breakfast mushroom – served with a fried duck's egg, an omelette or just sautéed and piled onto toast. For a vegetarian supper, pan-fry plenty of sliced St George's mushrooms until tender, adding a good handful of wild garlic leaves at the end – delicious whether you're vegetarian or not.

OMELETTE WITH ST GEORGE'S MUSHROOMS AND WILD GARLIC *serves* 4

A good non-stick frying pan is essential for successful omelettes. Gone are the days of proving your pan for hours on end with salt and oil.

90g butter

700–800g St George's mushrooms, cleaned and sliced (or left whole if small)

salt and freshly ground black pepper

handful of wild garlic leaves, washed, stalks removed and chopped

12 medium eggs, beaten

Melt about half of the butter in a hot frying pan. Add the St George's mushrooms, season and cook gently over a medium heat for 3–4 minutes or until they soften. Stir in the wild garlic leaves, then take off the heat and set aside; keep warm. Preheat the oven to 180°C/gas 4.

Beat the eggs in a bowl and season with salt and pepper. Rub a little butter over the bottom of a non-stick frying pan and heat gently, then add a quarter of the egg mixture. Stir with a rubber spatula or wooden spoon until the egg begins to set. Remove from the heat and slide the omelette flat onto a cold heatproof plate to prevent it cooking any further; set aside. Keep the omelettes a little undercooked to allow for reheating later. Repeat to make another 3 omelettes.

When all the omelettes are cooked, warm them through in the oven for a couple of minutes, then scatter the mushrooms and wild garlic on top. Serve at once.

CREAMED CHICKEN BROTH WITH ST GEORGE'S MUSHROOMS *serves* 4–6

There is something rather comforting about chicken and mushroom soup at any time of the year. If you've bought a whole free-range bird and just taken off the raw breasts for a dish, then this is the perfect way to use up the legs and carcass. All too often, not enough thought goes in to getting the best from a whole bird – they just tend to get roasted and that's it.

1 raw free-range chicken carcass, chopped

2 free-range chicken legs (or just the thighs or drumsticks)

1 onion, peeled and roughly chopped

1 leek, roughly chopped and washed

10 black peppercorns

1 bay leaf

a few sprigs of thyme

a few sprigs of tarragon, stalks separated, leaves roughly shredded

1½ litres good chicken stock

60g butter, plus an extra couple of knobs

50g plain flour

salt and freshly ground white pepper

100–120g St George's mushrooms, cleaned and sliced if large or halved or quartered

60ml double cream

Put the chicken carcass and legs into a pan with the onion, leek, peppercorns, bay leaf, thyme, tarragon stalks and stock. Bring to the boil, lower the heat and simmer gently for 35–40 minutes. Remove the chicken legs and set aside to cool. Strain the stock through a fine sieve.

Melt the 60g butter in a clean saucepan and stir in the flour. Cook, stirring, over a medium heat for a minute, then gradually add the strained stock, a ladleful at a time, stirring well to avoid lumps forming. Bring to the boil,

season and simmer gently for 30 minutes. Remove from
the heat. Blitz the soup using a free-standing or hand-
held stick blender to give it a nice silky finish. Return to
the cleaned pan.

Melt a couple of knobs of butter in a frying pan and
gently cook the mushrooms for 2—3 minutes without
colouring them. Remove the meat from the chicken legs
and shred into even-sized pieces with your fingers. Add to
the soup with the mushrooms, cream and tarragon leaves.
Taste and adjust the seasoning. Simmer gently for a
minute or so before serving.

BRAISED WILD RABBIT WITH
ST GEORGE'S MUSHROOMS *serves* 4

A rabbit makes for a cheap springtime meal and along with some seasonal, earthy mushrooms, the legs from two or three rabbits will easily serve four. Don't braise the rabbits' tender little saddle fillets with the legs; instead save them (in the freezer if you like) to pan-fry and use in a salad.

8 or 12 rabbit legs (use both front and back legs)

salt and freshly ground black pepper

40g plain flour, plus extra for dusting

vegetable oil for frying

80g butter

6 shallots, peeled and finely chopped

2 garlic cloves, peeled and crushed

100ml white wine or cider

1½ litres chicken stock (or a good stock cube dissolved in this amount of hot water)

200–250g St George's mushrooms, cleaned and sliced

3 tablespoons double cream

2 tablespoons chopped parsley

Chop the large back legs in half at the joint, using a heavy knife. Lightly season and flour the legs with a tablespoonful of the flour.

Heat a little oil in a heavy-based frying pan and lightly fry the rabbit legs for 2 minutes on each side, without colouring them too much. Remove and set aside.

Meanwhile, melt about 40g of the butter in a large heavy-based saucepan and gently cook the shallots with the garlic for 2–3 minutes until soft. Add the rest of the flour and stir well. Gradually add the wine, stirring well to avoid any lumps forming, and then add the chicken stock. Bring to the boil, stirring.

Add the rabbit legs to the pan and season lightly. Lower the heat, put the lid on and simmer gently for 1¼ hours or until the rabbit is very tender.

Meanwhile, melt the rest of the butter in the frying pan. Add the mushrooms, season lightly and cook gently for 4–5 minutes until they soften. Add to the rabbit legs with the cream and chopped parsley and simmer for another 5–6 minutes. Check the seasoning.

Serve with some good mashed potato and seasonal vegetables, such as spring greens.

Outdoor rhubarb

Outdoor rhubarb has the edge on the earlier forced rhubarb for me. It lends a wonderful, intense flavour to many desserts, and works well in savoury dishes too. I've cooked it with pork cheeks and found it gives a lovely sweet and sour finish to the sauce; you could do the same with duck or possibly pheasant.

Rhubarb makes a delicious crumble, tart or pie, served with lashings of real custard; or for a tangy cool dessert, fold cold rhubarb purée with whipped cream and cooled custard to make a fool. An abundance of rhubarb can be turned into a splendid jam – flavoured with ginger if you like. This is particularly good spread on toasted sourdough.

RHUBARB AND CUSTARD *serves 4–6*

Rhubarb and custard is a classic nursery pudding. Thick custard prepared with good quality ingredients is what really makes it.

FOR THE RHUBARB

400–500g rhubarb, trimmed and washed

120g caster sugar

FOR THE CUSTARD

300ml thick Jersey cream

½ vanilla pod, split lengthways

5 egg yolks

60g caster sugar

2 teaspoons cornflour

Preheat the oven to 200°C/gas 6 ready to bake the rhubarb.

To make the custard, pour the cream into a small saucepan. Scrape the seeds from the vanilla pod with the point of a knife and add them to the cream with the empty pod. Slowly bring to the boil, then remove from the heat and set aside to infuse for about 10 minutes.

Meanwhile, mix the egg yolks, sugar and cornflour together in a bowl. Pick out the vanilla pod, then pour the cream onto the egg mixture, mixing well with a whisk as you do so. Return to the pan and cook gently over a very low heat, stirring constantly with a wooden spoon, for a few minutes until the custard thickens; don't let it boil or it will curdle. Remove from the heat and give it a final mix with a whisk. Immediately pour into a clean bowl and leave to cool.

Cut the rhubarb roughly into 1cm pieces. Place in a baking tray or ovenproof dish and spoon over the sugar. Cover with foil and bake for about 30 minutes until the rhubarb is tender. Remove from the oven and carefully pour the cooking liquid into a saucepan. Boil the liquid until it has reduced by about half and thickened, then pour back over the rhubarb and leave to cool.

Serve the rhubarb warm or cold, topped with the thick warm or cold custard.

RHUBARB TARTS *serves 4*

This is based on the classic *tarte fine aux pommes* – the rhubarb works just as well as apples. It has proved to be a popular dessert, even when I've served it to friends who haven't been rhubarb lovers. Try to select stems that are bright red and of an even thickness, as the end result will look good.

150–200g ready-made all-butter
puff pastry

500–550g, deep red medium rhubarb
stalks, trimmed and washed

4 tablespoons caster sugar

FOR THE SYRUP
trimmings from the rhubarb

2 tablespoons caster sugar

FOR THE CREAM
100ml double or whipping cream

1 tablespoon caster sugar

Preheat the oven to 220°C/gas 7. Roll out the pastry to a 3mm thickness and cut four 12cm x 8cm rectangles. Lay on a non-stick or heavy baking tray, spacing them well apart.

Cut the rhubarb into 11cm lengths, reserving the trimmings for the syrup. Lay the rhubarb, side by side on the puff pastry rectangles, as close together as you can, leaving a ½cm margin free at the edges. Sprinkle the sugar evenly over the fruit and bake for 15–20 minutes until the pastry is crisp. The rhubarb shouldn't colour too much; if it appears to be doing so, turn the oven down to 190°C/gas 5.

Meanwhile, for the syrup, put the rhubarb trimmings into a pan along with the sugar. Heat slowly, then simmer gently for 8–10 minutes, stirring every so often. Strain the mixture through a fine sieve into a clean pan, pressing the pulp in the sieve with the back of a wooden spoon to extract as much juice as possible. (Set the rhubarb left in the sieve aside to cool.) Boil the rhubarb syrup until it has reduced by about half and thickened slightly. Remove from the heat and leave to cool.

Whip the cream with the sugar until thick, then carefully fold in about 1 tablespoon of the reserved rhubarb bits. (The rest can be discarded.)

Serve the rhubarb tarts warm on individual plates, with a spoonful of the flavoured cream and drizzled with some of the rhubarb syrup.

BUTTERMILK PUDDING WITH RHUBARB
serves 4

A compote of sharp, tangy rhubarb is the perfect foil for this light, creamy, vanilla-scented pudding. You could describe it as a British version of panna cotta.

10g leaf gelatine (3 large sheets)

350ml double cream

1 vanilla pod, halved lengthways

70g caster sugar

350ml buttermilk

FOR THE RHUBARB COMPOTE
250g young rhubarb, trimmed and cut into
2cm pieces

100g caster sugar

Soak the gelatine in a shallow dish of cold water for a few minutes to soften. Meanwhile, pour the cream into a small saucepan. Scrape the seeds from the vanilla pod and add them to the cream along with the empty pod and the sugar. Slowly bring to the boil, then remove from the heat. Squeeze out the excess water from the gelatine, then add to the cream mixture and stir until dissolved.

Leave to cool (but not set), then take out the vanilla pod. Whisk in the buttermilk, then strain the mixture. Pour into shallow individual moulds or coffee cups and leave to set in the fridge for 2–3 hours or overnight.

For the rhubarb compote, preheat the oven to 200°C/gas 6. Place the rhubarb in a shallow baking dish and scatter over the sugar. Cover with foil and bake for about 30 minutes until the rhubarb is soft.

Drain the liquor from the rhubarb into a saucepan and boil until it has reduced by half and thickened slightly. Stir back into the rhubarb and leave to cool.

To serve, dip the pudding moulds very quickly in and out of hot water, then turn out on to serving plates. Spoon the rhubarb compote around the puddings and serve at once.

VANILLA SUGAR

After you've used vanilla pods and extracted their seeds, you can still get flavour from the pods. Wash and dry them, then immerse in a standard sugar bowl of caster sugar. The pods will release their fragrance and you'll have a ready supply of vanilla sugar to use for ice creams and sauces.

May

Saltmarsh or Shetland LAMB, ASPARAGUS *plucked from the* Suffolk *marshes,* HERITAGE NEW POTATOES *not seen for a generation or so...*

OTHER INGREDIENTS NOT TO BE MISSED

Salmon   Sea trout   Razor clams   Welsh cockles   Rook   Gull's eggs   Sea beet   Sea kale

New season's garlic   Garlic leaves   St Georges's mushrooms   Pennywort

Purple-sprouting broccoli   Watercress   Outdoor rhubarb

May is the beginning of the green season for me – and I'm not talking Greenpeace and eco-friendly stuff here. Our own season for asparagus, peas, beans and leaves is about to begin and last a couple months or so, triggering off all those springtime culinary thoughts.

As much as I love freshly podded peas and beans, I haven't the time or patience to grow them at home. However, I do plant pea and mangetout seeds annually, purely for their shoots and young leaves. To me, this is much more satisfying and makes for delicious spring salads.

Asparagus is another much-loved ingredient I wouldn't attempt to grow, not in our garden. I'd rather support British growers than waste my time producing a few spears for the odd meal. I've always considered our growers are a bit hard done by, as they have to compete with cheap imports either side of a short season. I wouldn't mind paying a bit more for their produce either. Homegrown asparagus is too cheap for my liking and deserves the premium it has in countries like France and Germany.

Some lucky growers, though, have an advantage. At St Enedoc in Cornwall, Jax benefits from the Cornish microclimate and her asparagus is ready for eating by Easter. That's a month ahead of the usual season and most British growers, but who knows, with global warming our season may be due for an extension.

Along with grouse, asparagus is a food we should honour. The glorious 12TH August strikes a chord in foodies' minds, but asparagus deserves one hell of a celebration, too. I eat it at least a couple of times a week during its short season and when it's gone, it's gone. I don't resort to imported asparagus, except for white asparagus that is, which we can't seem to grow here for some reason.

Of course, May is also the start of the new potato season. When I was a kid, my gran made a huge thing of

Jersey Royals. She treated them like a luxury ingredient – serving them up on their own with butter and mint… they were always delicious. I suppose that's what it's all about – giving something seasonal and wonderful a special place on the table, as humble as it might be.

I never remember asparagus entering the house, though. Ours was a simple household, nothing posh, just honest, earthy ingredients and Grandad's homegrown tomatoes – loads of them – plus the occasional cucumber and melon from the greenhouse.

Of course, May is also the month when Jersey Royals appear in the shops. These days, some British potato growers are coming round to the fact that we can grow good new potatoes that give the Jersey farmers and foreign imports a run for their money. It's about time – after all a lot of the varieties we import were grown here centuries ago.

Another thing I remember as a kid is how often lamb appeared on the table. In those

days, I'd no idea what a best end was – I had never seen one. For us it was chops, liver, hearts and the occasional piece of slow-cooked breast. Undoubtedly my spring lamb recipes for this month have been influenced by these early experiences.

Look out for the less common ingredients that are in season, too. Gull's eggs are still around until the middle of this month. To capture their delicate qualities, boil for 7–8 minutes and serve simply with celery salt (see page 58) as a seasoning and mayonnaise (see page 119).

If you live near the coast and you're jumping on the foraging bandwagon – you'd be a fool not to – there's some great produce to be gathered for free during

May. Take a coastal walk in the right place and you'll find lots of tempting green seashore vegetables, like sea beet, wild fennel and sea purslane. Partner with poached or baked wild salmon if you want to splash out, or with any other simply cooked fish for that matter.

Sea kale is a great wild seashore vegetable if you know where to lay your hands on it. There is a cultivated variety on the market, but wild sea kale has a much better flavour and vibrant look – it is sometimes mistaken for sprouting broccoli.

Elvers, or baby eels, arrive in our rivers around May each year, but they are so rare now that they could soon be a thing of the past on restaurant menus. Because the eel population is so threatened, the majority of elvers are exported for breeding. For our menus we tend only to take the weaker ones that are unlikely to make the journey.

Sadly May is still rather fruitless, except for our outdoor rhubarb, which is great for crumbles, pies, fools and ice cream, of course. So some creative dessert-making is still needed this month before we can get stuck into those long-awaited summer fruits.

Asparagus

Hopefully you'll have avoided the temptation to buy imported asparagus through the rest of the year, as it is now time to appreciate our delicious native green spears.

There is so much you can do with asparagus, especially when there is a glut at the height of the season, although I favour simplicity and prefer to keep this prize vegetable as recognisable as possible.

It's hard to beat the classic pairing of steamed (or boiled) asparagus with hollandaise sauce, but it is also great scattered over simply grilled fish fillets, tossed into spring salads or piled onto warm toast. I also like to deep-fry the spears and serve them with wild garlic mayonnaise.

One of my favourite quirky dishes is a soft-boiled duck's egg with asparagus soldiers and celery salt. It's as simple a dinner party starter as you could wish to prepare, but fulfils that genius of marrying two ingredients in their purist and simplest form. If you boil a duck's egg for 4½–5 minutes and cook some asparagus spears for a similar amount of time then you've got it – you just need the celery salt (see page 58).

CHILLED ASPARAGUS AND SPRING HERB SOUP *serves 4–6*

If I've had to peel thick asparagus or only used the tips in a recipe, the trimmings never go in the bin. I've been using them to make this soup for years – it tastes slightly different each time, depending on the herbs I use. Feel free to vary the herbs, but I find that stronger ones like thyme, rosemary, coriander and tarragon are best avoided as they dominate and overwhelm the subtle fragrance of the soup.

If you grow your own herbs, this is the perfect way to use the prunings when the herbs start to bolt or get out of control. Last year I had an abundance of lovage, which is too overpowering for this soup, so I used a tempura batter to turn the leaves into fritters and served them as an accompaniment. Try it if you have some in your garden.

1 tablespoon vegetable oil

1 medium onion, peeled and roughly chopped

1 leek, trimmed, trimmed, roughly chopped and washed

1 tablespoon plain flour

1.5 litres vegetable stock

salt and freshly ground black pepper

a couple of good handfuls of asparagus trimmings or peelings, or a bargain bunch of asparagus, chopped

a handful of parsley, thicker stalks removed and reserved

a handful of chervil, washed, thicker stalks removed and reserved

a handful of basil, washed, thicker stalks removed and reserved

about 10g chives

a few mint leaves

TO SERVE (OPTIONAL)
finely chopped herbs, to garnish

cream, crème fraîche or soft goat's cheese

Heat the oil in a pan, add the onion and leek, then cover and cook gently for 4–5 minutes until soft, stirring every so often. Add the flour and stir well, then gradually add the vegetable stock and seasoning. Bring to the boil.

Add the asparagus peelings (or spears) to the pan, along with the reserved thicker herb stalks and simmer gently for 20 minutes. Add the rest of the herbs and simmer for a further 2 minutes, no longer.

Whiz the soup in a blender until smooth, then strain through a medium strainer (not a fine-meshed one, which would take out some of the herb bits) into a bowl. Set this over another bowl of iced water to cool the soup down as quickly as possible – this helps to keep its fresh green colour. Cover and chill until ready to serve.

Taste the soup and adjust the seasoning before serving. Divide among chilled bowls. If you like, garnish with finely chopped herbs and a dollop of cream or crème fraîche, or even a spoonful of fresh goat's cheese.

ASPARAGUS HOLLANDAISE *serves 4 as a starter*

This is a classic way to serve asparagus. Although not strictly British, hollandaise is one of those must-have sauces with hot asparagus. You'll need to allow around 250g unprepared weight per person. Asparagus is normally sold in 500g bunches, so buy one for every two people, but watch out – the wrapper can cleverly conceal woody stalks.

1kg medium asparagus

salt

FOR THE HOLLANDAISE
40ml white wine vinegar

40ml water

1 small shallot, peeled and chopped

a few sprigs of tarragon

1 bay leaf

5 peppercorns

200g unsalted butter

3 small egg yolks

freshly ground white pepper

For the hollandaise, put the wine vinegar, water, shallot, herbs and peppercorns into a small pan and reduce the liquid by boiling for a few minutes until there is no more than a dessertspoonful. Strain the liquor through a sieve and leave to cool.

To clarify the butter, melt it slowly in a pan, then simmer for 5 minutes. Remove from the heat, leave to cool a little, then pour off the clarified butter that has separated from the whey; discard the whey. (Clarifying helps to keep the hollandaise thick.)

Put the egg yolks and half of the vinegar reduction in a small heatproof bowl (or double boiler if you have one). Set over a pan of gently simmering water and whisk, using a hand-held electric beater, until the mixture begins to thicken and become frothy. Slowly trickle in the

butter, whisking continuously. If the butter is added too quickly, the sauce will separate. When you've added two-thirds of the butter, taste the sauce and add a little more, or all, of the remaining vinegar reduction. Then add the rest of the butter. The sauce shouldn't be too vinegary, but the vinegar should just cut the oiliness of the butter. Season with salt and pepper to taste. Cover with cling film and leave in a warm, but not hot, place until needed. If necessary, the hollandaise can be reheated over a bowl of hot water and lightly whisked again before serving.

For the asparagus, bring a pan of well-salted water to the boil. Trim off the tough ends of the asparagus, then add to the pan. Cook in gently simmering salted water for 4–5 minutes or until just tender. Drain and arrange on warm plates.

Either spoon the hollandaise sauce over the tips of just-cooked asparagus, or serve separately in small bowls. Eat with your fingers; it tastes much better.

FRIED DUCK'S EGG WITH BROWN SHRIMPS AND SPRUE ASPARAGUS *serves 2*

Asparagus growers always have an abundance of the tiny, wiry spears that grow in among the thick stalks that everyone wants to buy. They are delicate and perfect for a summer brunch or lunch dish. Towards the end of the season, farmers may sell on the little skinny offshoots, which are just right with a fried egg, or partnered with something tasty like these brown shrimps, or *crevette gris* as they are known across the water. If you like the idea of the brown shrimps and can't find them, cheat by buying a tub of potted shrimps.

250g sprue or extra fine asparagus

salt and freshly ground black pepper

1 tablespoon olive oil

4 duck's eggs

a couple of generous knobs of butter (but not if using potted shrimps)

50g brown shrimps or tub of potted shrimps

Trim off the woody ends from the asparagus and cut the spears in half if they are long. Cook in boiling salted water for 2–3 minutes or until tender, then drain.

Heat the olive oil in a frying pan and lightly fry the eggs for a couple of minutes until the white has just set.

Meanwhile, melt the butter in a pan and add the shrimps (or just tip in the potted shrimps). Add the asparagus, season and warm for a minute or so until hot. Transfer the eggs to warm plates and season with salt and pepper. Spoon the asparagus, shrimps and butter on top and serve.

VARIATIONS Fried eggs are not just for breakfast, they can make really interesting starters and lunches. Try frying some baby squid or cuttlefish to serve with your fried duck's or hen's eggs – and use the ink as a dressing. Or serve your eggs on sautéed chicken livers and wild mushrooms... delicious.

ASPARAGUS TART *serves 4*

This tart makes a good starter, or light lunch with a salad; it's also ideal for a picnic. Buy good quality butter puff pastry if you can – it gives a much lighter result than standard supermarket ready-made puff.

300–350g ready-made all-butter puff pastry

plain flour for dusting

1 egg, beaten

1kg medium asparagus

salt and freshly ground black pepper

30g freshly grated mature cheese, such as Cheddar

50g butter, plus extra for greasing

Roll out the puff pastry on a lightly floured surface to a 3mm thickness and let it rest for 15 minutes. Cut 4 pastry rectangles, 14cm x 11cm and prick them all over with a fork, then lay on a baking tray.

From the rest of the pastry, cut 1cm wide strips, as long as you can. Brush the edges of the rectangles with egg and lay the pastry strips on top, trimming them as necessary, to form a rim on all four sides. Mark these raised edges by pressing half-moons with the blade of a knife, or using a pastry crimper, then brush with egg. Leave to rest in the fridge for 1 hour.

In the meantime, cut off the woody ends of the asparagus spears and discard. Then cut the top 10cm of the tips, reserving the stalks. Bring two pans of salted water to the boil. Cook the tips for 3–4 minutes until tender, then drain and refresh in cold water to stop them discolouring.

Cook the trimmings in the other pan for about 7–8 minutes until soft, then drain and whiz in a blender or food processor with the grated cheese and butter to a coarse purée. Season with salt and pepper to taste.

Preheat the oven to 160°C/gas 3. Bake the pastry cases for 7 minutes, then remove. Turn the oven up to 200°C/gas 6. Spread about a tablespoonful of the asparagus purée in the middle of each tart. Don't put in too much (save what you have left to use as a dip). Then lay the asparagus tips, as close together as you can, on the purée.

Cut some pieces of foil just large enough to cover the asparagus (but not the pastry edges) and butter them. Season the asparagus with salt and pepper and lay the foil, buttered-side down, on top. Bake the tarts for 15 minutes and serve immediately.

New potatoes

Up in Northumberland at Tiptoe farm in the River Till valley, Lucy and Anthony Carroll are taking the appeal of potatoes to a whole new level. They grow over 18 varieties of Heritage potatoes, each with different eating qualities for specific jobs in the kitchen.

Many of the potatoes date back to the late 1800s, with names like Dunbar Rover, Arran Victory and Edzell Blue. There are no gimmicks with Carroll's Heritage. Even the naturally blue-fleshed varieties are full of flavour – perfect to brighten up salads to shock your guests.

Of course, Jersey Royals and other great new potatoes are delicious tossed in butter and mint as an accompaniment, but there are other possibilities. Try crushing them with lots of chopped herbs and use as a base for simply cooked fish, meat and offal. Or turn warm, buttery potatoes into a great starter by topping them with flakes of smoked mackerel or salmon and, perhaps, a little freshly grated horseradish.

ILLUSTRATED ABOVE: Royal Kidney (top left); Sharpe's Express (top right); La Ratte (below left); Red Duke of York (below right)

SPRING BUBBLE AND SQUEAK *serves 4*

Bubble and squeak needn't be just for using up wintry leftovers. In fact, I'm much more likely to cook the green veg and potatoes from scratch at any time of the year. The dish is so good with grilled meats; it also makes a delicious breakfast, brunch or lightish lunch.

Peas and beans – broad, runner and bobby beans – are chopped up with leftover or freshly cooked new potatoes, along with some spring or summer greens, spring onions and green herbs, then pan-fried as patties.

125–150g cooked, peeled new potatoes

200g spring greens, cooked, drained

6 spring onions, trimmed

100g podded broad beans, cooked

100g podded peas, cooked

1 tablespoon chopped parsley

salt and freshly ground black pepper

2 tablespoons vegetable oil

Chop the potatoes, greens, spring onions and beans and place in a bowl with the peas. Add the chopped parsley, mix well and season with salt and pepper to taste.

Shape the mixture into 4 even-sized patties and flatten them slightly.

Heat the oil in a non-stick frying pan and cook the patties for 3–4 minutes on each side until golden. Drain on kitchen paper and serve straight away, or keep warm in a low oven until ready to serve.

LOBSTER AND JERSEY ROYAL SALAD
WITH BACON *serves 4 as a starter or light lunch*

Earthy new potatoes like Jerseys or Cornish Earlies are a perfect match to seafood. Try to buy a piece of good bacon for this salad, as pre-sliced bacon tends to be too thin.

Don't throw the lobster shells away once you've taken the meat out – use them to make a soup as you would crab shells or shellfish-infused oil (see page 123) to use as a dressing for salads or grilled fish or shellfish salads.

2 live lobsters, each about 500g

500g Jersey Royals or Cornish Earlies (or other new potatoes), peeled

salt and freshly ground black pepper

4 thick slices of rindless smoked streaky bacon

1 tablespoon vegetable oil

a handful of small salad leaves (silver sorrel, baby spinach, nasturtiums, flat leaf parsley, bittercress, land cress, etc.)

FOR THE COURT BOUILLON

1 onion, peeled and quartered

2 carrots, peeled and roughly chopped

1 bay leaf

a few sprigs of thyme

1 teaspoon fennel seeds

10 black peppercorns

a few parsley stalks

FOR THE DRESSING

1 tablespoon cider vinegar

4 tablespoons extra virgin rapeseed oil, or shellfish-infused oil (see page 123)

a few sprigs of tarragon

½ garlic clove

An hour or so before cooking the lobsters, place them in the freezer to make them sleepy (deemed to be the most humane way of preparing live lobsters for cooking).

To make the court bouillon: put all the ingredients into a saucepan (that will be large enough to take the lobsters). Cover with cold water, bring to the boil and simmer for 10 minutes. Drop the lobsters into the court bouillon, simmer for 5 minutes, then set aside to cool in the liquid.

Meanwhile, cook the new potatoes in boiling salted water for 12–15 minutes until just cooked. Drain and leave to cool.

When the lobsters are cool enough to handle, split them in half with a heavy chopping knife and remove the meat from the shell, reserving any juices. Cut the meat into bite-sized chunks. Crack the claws and leg joints with the back of the knife and take out the meat.

Whisk all of the ingredients together for the dressing and season with salt and pepper. Set aside.

Cut the bacon roughly into 5mm cubes. Heat the oil in a frying pan and fry the bacon for 3–4 minutes until crisp, then drain on kitchen paper.

Arrange the salad leaves, potatoes and lobster on serving plates. Strain the dressing and drizzle over the salad, dressing it well. Scatter over the bacon and serve.

VARIATIONS As an alternative to lobster, you can use the same weight of crayfish or Dublin Bay prawns for this salad. A handful of blanched homegrown asparagus is a great addition, too.

New season's lamb

Spring lamb is one of our great British meats – a must-have treat, especially if you can get your hands on Saltmarsh lamb, or the animals that feed on seaweed in the Shetland Isles. As you can imagine this grazing, at low tide, has a tremendous impact on flavour and the meat is very special.

Simple cooking methods are the best options for spring lamb. Only the breast calls for long slow cooking (see recipe overleaf). Simply roast leg, loin or rack of spring lamb, and griddle or pan-fry cutlets and leg steaks, then serve with a sympathetic seasonal partner. For example, try a twist on a classic mint sauce by adding other chopped spring herbs, such as chervil and parsley, or make a pesto-like sauce using wild garlic leaves, walnuts and olive oil.

Don't always go for the obvious cuts either. Neck fillets are much more tender than those from an older animal and can be treated almost like loin fillets. Serve them grilled with asparagus and new potatoes, or sliced and tossed in a salad. Do check though that the meat you are getting from your butcher is definitely spring lamb and he is not palming you off with last season's… or you will be in for a bit of a surprise.

LAMB CUTLETS WITH REDCURRANT JELLY *serves* 4

Serve these breaded cutlets as a main course, or at a drinks party – they're easy to eat with your fingers. You can also treat mutton cutlets the same way, as the best end is the most tender of all the mutton cuts. Now is the time to use the last of the redcurrant jelly you made last summer, or buy a jar of good quality ready-made.

12 best end lamb cutlets, chined and excess fat trimmed

salt and freshly ground black pepper

plain flour for dusting

2 eggs, beaten

50–60g fresh white breadcrumbs

vegetable oil for shallow-frying

a couple of knobs of butter

redcurrant jelly, to serve

Flatten the cutlets a little with the palm of your hand and season them. Have three shallow bowls ready, one containing the flour, one with the beaten eggs and one with the breadcrumbs.

Pass the cutlets first through the flour to dust all over, shaking off any excess, then dip in the beaten eggs and finally into the breadcrumbs, turning to coat them evenly on all sides.

Heat about a 1cm depth of oil in a deep, heavy-based frying pan over a medium heat. When it is hot, add the cutlets and fry for about 3–4 minutes on each side until golden, adding the butter a couple of minutes after turning them. Drain on kitchen paper.

Serve the breaded cutlets immediately, accompanied by redcurrant jelly.

MIXED GRILL OF LAMB WITH ROSEMARY AND SPRING BUBBLE AND SQUEAK *serves 4*

A simple mixed grill has its merits on the dinner table. You can use your favourite prime cuts – cutlets, saddle fillets or noisettes – and mix in a bit of offal according to your taste. If you're cooking for a lot of guests, you can fry the thicker cuts to start with, keeping them nice and rare, and finish them under the grill while you pan-fry the kidneys and liver quickly at the last minute.

4 lamb cutlets or loin chops (or both)

salt and freshly ground black pepper

3–4 tbsp vegetable oil

2 lamb's hearts, quartered and sinews removed

8 plump lamb's sweetbreads

4 lamb's kidneys, halved and sinews removed

4 slices of lamb's liver, about 1cm thick

a couple of generous knobs of butter

handful of rosemary leaves

handful of wild garlic leaves (optional)

TO SERVE

spring bubble and squeak (see page 79)

Season the lamb cutlets or chops with salt and pepper. Heat a ridged griddle pan or heavy-based frying pan, brush with oil and cook the cutlets or chops for about 3 minutes on each side, keeping them rare. Transfer to a baking tray.

Cook the hearts in the same way and place on the tray. Season the sweetbreads and fry over a high heat for about 3–4 minutes, then place on the tray.

Preheat the grill to high. Finish the pan-fried meats under the grill for about 4–5 minutes to colour them nicely, turning after a couple of minutes. Meanwhile, season the kidneys and heat a little more oil in the pan if you need to. Griddle or fry the kidneys for a couple of minutes on each side, keeping them pink; do the same with the liver, allowing a little less time.

Heat the butter in a small frying pan until foaming. Throw in the rosemary, and wild garlic if using, and stir over the heat for about 30 seconds.

Arrange the meats on a large serving dish or individual plates with the bubble and squeak, spoon over the rosemary and wild garlic butter, and serve at once.

SPRING LAMB SALAD
serves 4 as a starter, 2 as a main course

For this salad, you can use any combination of your favourite lamb cuts and offal – cooked pink and sliced up. Slow-cooked belly – pan-fried until crisp, shredded and scattered over the salad is a great addition. I like to use salad leaves and herbs from the garden – flat leaf parsley, chervil and bittercress with a little mint works well. And as your garden develops, you may want to add some pea shoots, rocket leaves, chives and other small salad leaves, or perhaps even some peas and beans later in the season.

2 pieces of spring lamb neck fillet, about 200g in total

salt and freshly ground black pepper

1 tablespoon vegetable oil

2–3 slices of lamb's liver, 120–150g in total

a few slices of roasted stuffed breast of lamb (see page 84), optional

a couple of handfuls of small salad and herb leaves (flat leaf parsley, chervil, bittercress, mint, etc.)

FOR THE DRESSING

2 tablespoons good quality white wine vinegar

1 teaspoon grain mustard

a few mint leaves

6–7 tablespoons olive oil

Season the lamb fillet with salt and pepper. Heat the oil in a frying pan and fry the pieces of fillet for about 4–5 minutes on each side until pink. Remove from the pan and set aside on a warm plate to rest.

For the dressing, whiz all the ingredients together in a blender and season to taste.

Just before serving, fry the lamb's liver slices in the pan over a high heat for about 30 seconds on each side, then remove and cut into strips. Briefly warm the slices of cooked breast if using.

To serve, toss the leaves in the dressing and arrange on serving plates. Slice the lamb fillet and arrange on top, with the liver and roasted stuffed breast if using.

STUFFED BREAST OF LAMB *serves 4–6*

Breast of lamb is one of those cuts that invariably ends up in the butcher's bin these days. I doubt whether many butchers even bother trimming the small amount of meat to put it through the mincer. However, there are a few good things you can do with the breast.

The simplest way to cook it is to slow-roast it until crisp, then slice it up and snack on it or scatter it into a salad. Lamb scrumpets – strips of breast simmered until tender, then crumbed and fried – are also delicious and make a great, cheap snack to go with drinks.

Last year, when I was down on Alex James' farm in Gloucestershire, we played around with a lot of different cuts, but it was the stuffed, slow-cooked breast that had the best flavour, for sure.

Here I've included the offal, both in the stuffing and pan-fried to top the dish and finish it off.

1 breast of lamb, boned

salt and freshly ground black pepper

splash of cider or water

120–150g lamb's sweetbreads

2 lamb's kidneys

a couple of generous knobs of butter

1 tablespoon chopped parsley

FOR THE STUFFING

1 onion, peeled and finely chopped

2 garlic cloves, peeled and crushed

1 teaspoon chopped thyme leaves

1 teaspoon chopped rosemary leaves

2 tablespoons olive oil

120g lamb mince

100g lamb's liver, coarsely minced or chopped

3–4 lamb's sweetbreads, cut into small dice

2 lamb's kidneys, sinews removed and cut into small dice

50g fresh white breadcrumbs

Preheat the oven to 220°C/gas 7. To make the stuffing, gently cook the onion, garlic, thyme and rosemary in the olive oil for 3–4 minutes until soft. Transfer to a bowl, add the rest of the ingredients, season generously and mix well.

Lay the breast of lamb, skin side down, on a work surface or board and spoon the stuffing down the centre, then roll it up tightly. Tie with string at 3–4cm intervals, season and lay in a roasting tray. Roast in the oven for 20 minutes, then lower the setting to 180°C/gas 4 and cook for another 1½ hours. Set aside to rest for about 10 minutes. Deglaze the roasting pan with a little cider and reserve the juices.

Meanwhile, blanch the sweetbreads in lightly salted water for 1 minute, then drain. Remove any sinew or fat and cut the larger ones in half. Remove any sinews from the kidneys and cut into similar-sized pieces. Season both with salt and pepper.

Heat the butter in a heavy-based frying pan until foaming. Add the sweetbreads and kidneys and fry for 3–4 minutes over a high heat until nicely coloured. Add the parsley and remove from the heat.

To serve, slice the breast of lamb into 2cm thick slices and arrange on plates, then spoon the offal around the meat and pour over the pan juices. Serve with spring greens and mash, or colcannon. Save any leftover roast for lamb baps or sandwiches.

June

Wild seashore VEGETABLES, CRAYFISH *fished from our* rivers *and* ponds, *fresh oily* MACKEREL *from the sea, and fragrant* ELDERFLOWERS *gathered from* hedgerows

OTHER INGREDIENTS NOT TO BE MISSED

Salmon   Sea trout   Lobster   Lamb   Gull's eggs

Asparagus   Broad beans   Peas   Runner beans   Wild fennel   Courgette flowers   Nasturtiums

Rhubarb   Wild strawberries   Strawberries   Gooseberries   Raspberries   Cherries

June is the month when I'll start to have an abundance of herbs and salad leaves in the garden, weather permitting of course. I pick these as I need them, tossing them into all kinds of summery dishes to add variety, but there are plenty more seasonal treats to look out for now. Elderflowers, for example, are in blossom. It's well worth harvesting thesc to make a concentrated syrup or cordial, which can be stored for use later in the year. The great thing with elderflower syrup is that you can make it as concentrated as you like and use it for jellies and all kinds of creamy puddings, or simply as a refreshing summer drink – with or without alcohol.

There is rarely a time on a country or coastal walk when I don't get tempted to forage for wild plants, berries or fungi – I mean it's like ignoring free food. This is a particularly good time to gather seashore veg. As a kid I was oblivious to these common vegetables, but I've really got into them over the last few years. Learning to appreciate true wild flavours must be part of growing up.

Whenever I am on the coast, I cannot resist filling a carrier bag with edible samphire, sea spinach or sea beet, sea purslane and sea kale. Samphire starts to show its tender green stems on seashore marshes at this time of year and is the perfect accompaniment to fish dishes.

It's actually very easy to forage for yourself, but you do need to be careful as there are restrictions on some National Trust coastal strips. If you live a long way from the coast, then samphire may not be accessible, unless you have a good greengrocer, farmers' market or fishmonger to source it for you.

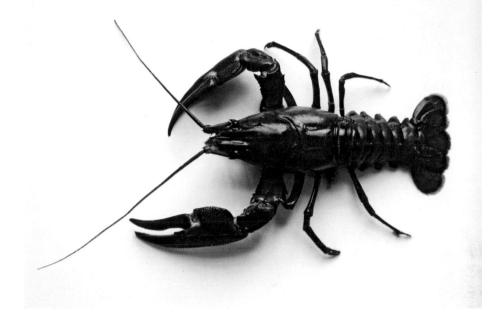

Mackerel are starting to scavenge at this time of the year, so if you're out fishing on the coast, be sure to pack some mackerel feathers or lures in case the bass (or whatever you are fishing for) aren't biting. These are strings of six hooks, each with a feather attached to attract the fish, so if you're really lucky you might catch half a dozen in one go. Once you hit a shoal of mackerel, you'll fill a carrier bag in no time.

As a child, I lived right on the seafront in West Dorset and could see the shoals move into the beach from my window. I'd have my simple rod with its single hook set up in no time and learnt what mackerel was all about when it was eaten more or less straight out of the water. It was so fresh it would curl up in the pan unless we butterflied it first. Simple grilled, pan-fried or soused mackerel make a delicious supper, but these days I'm just as fussy about the freshness of my mackerel and can detect any slightly sour tinge before it hits my lips.

This is also a good month to focus on crayfish as they lend themselves to great salads and sandwiches for picnics, etc. There is some confusion over these freshwater crustacea that look like mini-lobsters.

When I was a kid, our local fishermen would land the occasional seawater crawfish (the clawless rock lobster), which they always referred to as crayfish. In Australia the same name is used for these saltwater crustaceans. But here it is the freshwater creatures that we mean when we talk about crayfish.

Sadly we have lost most of our natives as the American signal crayfish, which were introduced in the early 1970s, have killed off most of ours. It seemed a sensible move at the time, because the American signals were immune to a disease that was devastating our crayfish. Little did anyone realise the havoc they would cause. Not only have the signals virtually wiped out our native white-clawed crayfish, but they are causing a hell of a lot of destruction to our rivers, ponds and reservoirs. They are prolific breeders, too. Even worse, they don't just stay put in one river or reservoir, they have the ability to move across land and populate and breed in new waters. And this is why we need to eat more of them, rather than import Turkish and Chinese crayfish to sustain our high street sandwich bars. Keen to promote them, I started my own little East End crayfish feast last year for foodies, food writers and others… let's hope it takes off.

As for other produce, it is time to make the most of the final asparagus now, also to pick the first green beans and peas. And, at last, we can enjoy a simple fruit salad of our homegrown berries. Cherries from Kent are a simple pleasure in themselves… don't miss out.

Wild seashore vegetables

The seashore and surrounding areas are rife with lots of edible plants like sea beet, sea cabbage, samphire and rock samphire, sea purslane and many more. I've even been introduced to sea peas, which are delicious in a salad if you pick the tiny shoots. And we don't have to wait until delicious crunchy samphire appears in the summer, for we can enjoy sea spinach and sea purslane all the year round.

These wild seashore vegetables can be used, both individually and combined, in a variety of ways – from pickling to simple steaming. A piece of freshly caught fish, such as pollack or gurnard, is at its best scattered with simple steamed or blanched seashore vegetables.

Samphire is particularly good with fish, but you can also fold it into omelettes, toss it into salads or deep-fry it as a snack.

Sea spinach is a much tastier alternative to leaf spinach and has a far better texture. Some of the stronger-tasting sea vegetables like rock samphire (not to be confused with marsh samphire) are perfect for pickling and serving with, say, smoked fish.

Next time you go for a coastal walk, keep your eyes open for these wild sea vegetables and take a carrier bag with you – it won't take you long to fill it.

ILLUSTRATED OPPOSITE: samphire (top left); rock samphire (top right); sea purslane (below left); sea spinach (below right)

DEEP-FRIED SAMPHIRE *serves 4*

After visiting Japan and eating tempura at Japanese restaurants in London, it dawned on me that samphire must be delicious deep-fried – a bit like the famous shredded zucchini they serve at Harry's Bar in Venice. And it is… perfect as a snack, starter or side dish for fish. If you can get your hands on some fresh Morecambe bay shrimps in the shell, coat them in the batter and deep-fry them with the samphire for a really tasty starter.

> 150g samphire
> vegetable oil for deep-frying
> lemon wedges, to serve
> FOR THE BATTER
> 60g self-raising flour
> salt
> pinch of cayenne pepper
> about 100ml ice-cold light beer or lager

Trim any woody stalks from the samphire, wash well and dry thoroughly. To make the batter, put the flour, salt and cayenne pepper into a bowl and gently whisk in the beer to form a smooth batter.

Meanwhile, heat the oil in a deep-fat fryer or heavy-based pan to 160°C. Now comes the messy bit: a handful at a time, plunge the samphire into the batter and make sure all the stems are coated, then remove and drain off the excess batter, letting it run through your fingers.

Deep-fry the samphire in batches: carefully drop a few pieces into the oil, stirring the oil with a slotted spoon to keep them separate, and deep-fry until crispy. Drain on kitchen paper and keep warm while you cook the rest. Serve straight away, with lemon wedges.

VARIATION Cougette flowers, or rather immature courgettes with their flowers attached, are around this month and can be deep-fried in the same way until crisp and golden for a stunning starter.

STEAMED COCKLES WITH BACCHUS AND SAMPHIRE *serves 4 as a starter or lunch*

If you can find them, large fresh cockles are a real treat – as good as any clams. The problem with cockles is their gritty reputation, acquired from those little tubs of mass-produced cockles you can buy along with crabsticks and prawn shapes. Clearly there isn't the same attention paid to pre-cook washing in the factories that a chef would assign.

To clean cockles properly, you need to leave them under running water for about 15 minutes, agitating them every so often with your hands to release any sand which tends to get trapped in the grooves of the shell.

Here I've cooked them in a British wine made from the Bacchus grape, which seems to cope well with our climate. Although our winemakers have never really competed with their European counterparts, I'd recommend the white wines from the Chapel Down Bacchus vineyard in Kent and The Coddington vineyard up in Herefordshire. They are very good with seafood and, as here, adding a splash during cooking works a treat.

> 1.5kg plump, fresh cockles
> handful (or more) of samphire, washed
> a few generous knobs of butter
> 4 shallots, peeled, halved and thinly sliced
> 2 garlic cloves, peeled and crushed
> salt and freshly ground black pepper
> 100ml white wine (preferably English Bacchus)
> 100ml water

Wash the cockles (as described above) and drain. Trim any woody stalks from the samphire and set aside.

Heat the butter in a large pan and gently cook the shallots and garlic for 2–3 minutes until softened. Add the drained cockles, season with salt and pepper, then pour in the wine and water. Cover with a tight-fitting lid and cook over a medium-high heat for about 2–3 minutes, shaking the pan frequently.

Add the samphire and cook for another 2–3 minutes until the cockle shells have opened; discard any that remain shut. Serve immediately.

ROAST POLLACK WITH SEASHORE VEGETABLES AND OYSTER BUTTER *serves 4*

If you're a fisherman and forager, this dish could cost you next to nothing. You can use some or all of the sea vegetables listed, according to what is available. You can always improvise with, say, some baby spinach leaves, chard or cultivated sea kale, but don't expect it to have the flavour of its wild cousin. Sea beet tastes the way shop-bought spinach should – full of iron and slightly robust. Like chard, the leaves have a thick white stem, which can be left on or removed if you prefer.

As a kid I'd catch large pollack from offshore wrecks. There wasn't a market for it then; even now it's rarely seen on restaurant menus or fishmongers' slabs. Pollack is, however, a great sustainable alternative to our endangered cod, and large pollack are comparable in flavour and texture. Try to buy fillets from a pollack that weighed at least 2–3kg, as the flesh on smaller fish tends to be flaky.

200g sea kale, trimmed

salt and freshly ground black pepper

2 handfuls of small sea beet leaves, trimmed and washed

2–3 handfuls of tender, green sea purslane leaves

2 handfuls of samphire (optional)

2 tablespoons vegetable or rapeseed oil

4 pollack fillets, each 160–200g, skinned

a good knob of butter

FOR THE OYSTER BUTTER

2 rock oysters

2 shallots, peeled and roughly chopped

½ glass of white wine (preferably English)

½ glass of water

juice of ½ lemon

150g cold butter, diced

First make the oyster butter. Shuck the oysters, saving the juices. Put the shallots in a small pan with the white wine and water and simmer for a couple of minutes until the liquor has reduced by two-thirds. Add the oysters with their juice and the lemon juice. Remove from the heat and whiz in a blender until smooth. Return to the pan, place on a low heat and whisk in the butter, a few pieces at a time, to form a smooth sauce. Set aside.

Cut the sea kale into small pieces (4–5cm), discarding any thick stalks. Add to a pan of boiling salted water and cook for 3–4 minutes until tender, then drain and put into a bowl. Blanch the sea beet in boiling salted water for 30 seconds, then drain and add to the bowl. Blanch the sea purslane for 30 seconds, drain and add to the other blanched vegetables. If you're using samphire, trim any woody stalks and blanch for 10 seconds in boiling water, drain and mix with the rest of the vegetables.

Meanwhile, heat the oil in a heavy-based frying pan. Season the fish fillets and cook them, skin side down first, for 3–4 minutes on each side depending on their thickness; thinner fillets from smaller fish will need a little less. Add the knob of butter as you turn the fish.

Dress the sea vegetables with some of the oyster butter and season. Divide about two-thirds of them among warm plates and place the fish fillets on top. Scatter the rest of the sea vegetables on top and spoon over more oyster butter to serve.

SAMPHIRE OMELETTE *serves 2*

The fresh, slight saltiness of samphire helps to perk up an omelette, whether it's for breakfast, brunch or lunch. For a special touch, add some shellfish, such as freshly cooked prawns, white crab meat, mussels, etc., as you serve the omelette. A good non-stick frying pan is essential.

100g (or more) samphire, washed

50g butter

4 spring onions, trimmed and finely chopped

salt and freshly ground black pepper

6 medium eggs

Remove any woody stalks from the samphire. Melt half the butter in a hot frying pan. Add the spring onions and half the samphire, season and cook quickly over a medium heat for a minute or so. Set aside; keep warm.

Beat the eggs in a bowl and season with salt and pepper, then mix in the cooked spring onions and samphire. Preheat the oven to 180°C/gas 4.

Rub a little butter over the bottom of a non-stick frying pan and heat gently, then add half the egg mixture. Stir with a rubber spatula or wooden spoon until the egg begins to set. Remove from the heat and slide the omelette flat onto a cold heatproof plate to prevent it cooking any further. Keep the omelette a little undercooked, as you'll be reheating it later. Repeat to make the second omelette.

Heat the remaining butter in a pan and cook the rest of the samphire over a low heat for a minute or so, without colouring. Warm the omelettes through in the oven for a couple of minutes, then scatter the warm samphire on top and serve.

Crayfish

Crayfish call for a cooking liquid that is more strongly flavoured than saltwater shellfish do. The secret is to use a lot of aromatics, preferably of the fennel and aniseed family – wild fennel is perfect. A large dose of wine or beer helps too, along with plenty of sea salt.

TO COOK THE CRAYFISH: Bring a litre or so of beer or white wine to the boil, add 2 cupfuls of water, 1 tablespoon fennel seeds, some black peppercorns, 2–3 heaped tablespoons sea salt and 2 handfuls of wild fennel stalks. You can save the leaves to chop up and serve with the crayfish if you like. Let the liquor simmer for 5 minutes, then plunge in the crayfish. Bring back to the boil and simmer for 2–3 minutes, then remove from the liquid and leave to cool.

If you are serving them simply, a good mayonnaise (see page 119) is the ideal complement. A watercress mayonnaise goes brilliantly with crayfish, probably because the two have a synergy with clean streams. Blanch a good handful of trimmed watercress in boiling salted water for 30 seconds, then refresh in cold water, drain and squeeze out the excess water. Blend or finely chop the watercress, then stir into mayonnaise.

An apple mayonnaise is equally good. Simmer around 150ml good quality apple juice, such as Chegworth, until concentrated down to a tablespoon or so, cool, then whisk into some mayonnaise. Or flavour with a dash of apple brandy instead.

TO SHELL THE CRAYFISH: Remove the head and then squeeze the shell between your thumb and forefinger to crack it, so you can take out the tail meat in one piece. Don't discard the shells though – use them to make a soup or flavouring oil in the same way that you would crab shells (see page 123).

POTTED CRAYFISH ON TOAST *serves 4–6*

Last year at our crayfish feast we had too many peeled crayfish tails left, so I thought I'd adapt our potted shrimp recipe to serve with pre-feast drinks. It worked a treat.

180g unsalted butter

juice of ½ lemon

a good pinch of ground mace or nutmeg

pinch of cayenne pepper

1 small bay leaf

1 teaspoon anchovy essence or paste

about 200g cooked, peeled crayfish tails

salt and freshly ground white pepper

TO SERVE

hot buttered toast

2 lemons, halved

Melt the butter in a pan and add the lemon juice, mace, cayenne pepper, bay leaf and anchovy essence. Simmer over a low heat for 2 minutes to infuse the butter with the spices, then pour into a bowl and leave to cool until it is just warm.

Add the peeled crayfish and stir well, then season with salt and white pepper to taste. Cover and chill, stirring every so often, until the butter starts to set. Spoon the mixture into 4 ramekins or directly onto plates if serving straight away.

If preparing ahead, cover the ramekins with cling film and refrigerate, but remove from the fridge around 30 minutes before serving to bring to room temperature.

Serve the potted crayfish with hot buttered toast and lemon halves for squeezing.

RABBIT AND CRAYFISH STARGAZY PIE

serves 4–6

Like everyone else, I'm keen to do my bit for the environment and sustainability was the thinking behind this pie. Rabbits and crayfish are doing their fair share to ruin crops and destroy other water life, so it makes sense to eat more of them to keep them under control. You might remember seeing me preparing this dish on *Great British Menu* – it certainly proved to be popular!

24 live freshwater crayfish

8 wild rabbit legs, boned and cut into rough 2cm chunks

salt and freshly ground black pepper

3 tablespoons plain flour

2–3 tablespoons vegetable oil

2 onions, peeled and finely chopped

a good knob of butter

1 glass of white wine

3 litres hot good chicken stock

2 tablespoons double cream

1 tablespoon chopped parsley

1 teaspoon chopped tarragon

TO FLAVOUR THE CRAYFISH LIQUOR

1 teaspoon fennel seeds

12 black peppercorns

a few sprigs of thyme

2 star anise

1 bay leaf

FOR THE PASTRY

225g self-raising flour

1 teaspoon salt

85g shredded beef suet

60g butter, chilled and coarsely grated

1 medium egg, beaten, plus extra to glaze

150–175ml water

plain flour for dusting

Put the crayfish into the freezer for about an hour (to make them sleepy). Season the rabbit and dust with a little of the flour. Heat the oil in a heavy-based frying pan and lightly brown the rabbit pieces, then remove and set aside.

In another pan, gently cook the onions in the butter for 2–3 minutes without colouring. Dust with the remaining flour and stir well over a low heat for a minute. Gradually stir in the wine and 2 litres of the hot chicken stock, stirring to avoid lumps forming. Bring to the boil, then add the pieces of rabbit and season lightly with salt and pepper. Cover and simmer gently for about an hour until the rabbit is tender.

Meanwhile, bring a large pan of water (big enough to hold all the crayfish) to the boil with the fennel seeds, peppercorns, thyme, star anise, bay leaf and 2 tablespoons salt added. Simmer for 5 minutes. Plunge the crayfish into the boiling liquor, bring back to the boil and simmer for 1½ minutes, then drain and leave to cool.

Pick out 4 similar-sized crayfish for the garnish and shell the rest, including any large claws, first removing the head and then squeezing the shell between your thumb and forefinger to crack it. Put the meat aside. Crush up the shells a little and put them into a saucepan with the rest of the chicken stock. Bring to the boil and simmer for 30 minutes, then blitz in a blender and strain through a fine sieve into a clean pan. Let the stock bubble until reduced to about 4–5 tablespoons, then add the cream and reduce again, by half.

Once the rabbit is cooked the liquor should be quite thick. If not, uncover, remove the pieces of rabbit and let the liquor bubble for a while until reduced and thickened, then return the rabbit. Pour in the reduced crayfish liquor and stir in the parsley, tarragon and crayfish tails. Fill a large pie dish or 4 individual ones with the mixture.

To make the pastry, mix the flour, salt and suet together in a bowl. Add the grated butter and rub with your fingertips until you have a fine breadcrumb-like consistency. Mix in the beaten egg and enough of the water to form a smooth dough, then knead for a minute.

Roll out on a lightly floured surface to about a 5mm thickness. Trim until about 2cm larger all the way round than the rim of the pie dish (or cut discs for individual dishes). Brush the edges of the pastry with a little of the beaten egg. Lay the pastry over the filling, pressing the egg-washed sides onto the rim of the dish(es). Cut a small slit in the top of the pie(s) and insert the 4 whole crayfish so the top half of the body sits proud of the pastry, then brush the pastry with beaten egg. You can put a trim around the edge of the dish with a strip of leftover pastry if you like. Leave to rest in a cool place for about 30 minutes.

Preheat the oven to 200°C/gas 6. Bake for 45 minutes or until the pastry is golden brown (allow 10–15 minutes less for individual pies). Serve at once.

Mackerel

The great thing with mackerel is that they are cheap, tasty and need little doing to them – perfect for a barbecue, as a squeeze of lemon, good bread and a simple tomato or leafy salad is all you'll need. They respond well to baking and grilling, too. And when really fresh, mackerel makes top-notch sashimi – these days a sharp knife, soy and wasabi go into my tackle bag when I'm fishing for them. As they're probably the easiest of all fish to catch, you might well end up with too many for supper. Panic not though, you can souse your excess catch to make it last a week, or just surprise your neighbours with a fishy gift.

PAN-FRIED MACKEREL WITH GREEN TOMATO AND LOVAGE RELISH *serves* 4

Green tomatoes have an acidity that works perfectly with the oiliness of mackerel. If you're a tomato grower, you may well have some green tomatoes on your vines that you could tempt off for this relish, or perhaps you grow one of the heritage varieties designed to be eaten green. If not, your greengrocer might be able to oblige.

4 large mackerel fillets (with skin), or 8 smaller ones, trimmed

salt and freshly ground black pepper

1–2 tablespoons plain flour for dusting

1 tablespoon vegetable or corn oil

FOR THE RELISH

4 large green tomatoes

4 tablespoons rapeseed oil

1 onion, peeled and finely chopped

1 tablespoon cider vinegar

1 tablespoon caster sugar

a few lovage leaves, shredded

First make the relish. Halve the tomatoes, squeeze out the seeds, then roughly chop the flesh. Heat the rapeseed oil in a pan and gently cook the onion for 4–5 minutes, stirring regularly, until softened. Add the cider vinegar and sugar and simmer, stirring, for a minute.

Add the chopped tomatoes to the pan, season with salt and pepper, and continue cooking for 2–3 minutes, stirring regularly. Remove from the heat, stir in the lovage and leave to cool.

Check the mackerel fillets for any pin bones, then score the skin side 3 or 4 times. Season with salt and pepper and lightly flour the skin side only. Heat the oil in a non-stick frying pan. Cook the fillets, skin side down first, for 3–4 minutes on each side depending on the size of the fillets.

Serve at once, with the green tomato and lovage relish.

BARBECUED OR GRIDDLED MACKEREL WITH WILD FENNEL *serves* 4

If you are barbecuing on the beach, mackerel are the perfect fish to cook, especially if you've caught them yourself. Wild fennel is a prolific wild herb with fern-like leaves, which can be found growing in most seaside locations – you just need to know what to look for. It's perfect for stuffing whole fish like mackerel and sea bass, or for chopping into a sauce, salad or dressing.

A salad of wafer-thin fennel is a great accompaniment and you can always make it ahead and pack it into a plastic container for a beach barbecue or picnic.

4 small whole mackerel, heads removed and gutted

salt and freshly ground white pepper

vegetable oil for brushing

2 handfuls of wild fennel

FOR THE FENNEL SALAD

1 fennel bulb, trimmed, feathery fronds reserved

2 tablespoons good quality cider vinegar

1 tablespoon extra virgin rapeseed oil

First prepare the salad. Quarter the fennel bulb then, using a mandolin or very sharp knife, shred it as finely as possible. Tip into a bowl, add the cider vinegar and some salt and white pepper, and toss to mix. Leave to stand for 30 minutes. Roughly chop the reserved fennel fronds.

Drain off most of the vinegar from the salad and add the rapeseed oil and chopped fennel fronds. Toss well.

Heat up the barbecue or ridged griddle pan. Score the mackerel 4 or 5 times across their width through the skin, season with salt and pepper and brush with a little oil. Stuff the wild fennel into the cavities. Cook the mackerel on the barbecue or griddle pan over a medium heat for 5–6 minutes on each side. Serve with the fennel salad.

Elderflowers

Elderflowers normally start appearing in mid-June, depending on the part of the country in which you live. Like seashore vegetables, they are food for free – just waiting to be picked. It's a great excuse to get the kids out into the countryside and learn that they can gather food for free. It's also important to give them a healthy, natural drinking option that is not full of chemicals.

A few bottles of simple, strong elderflower syrup made at the height of the season should last you through the year – to use as a base for a refreshing cordial, cocktail or elderflower Champagne.

The subtle flavour and perfume of elderflower is a great addition to creamy desserts, like flummeries and fools. You can also make a delicious elderflower jelly with the diluted syrup – suspending whatever fruits you fancy in it and setting it with gelatine.

Elderflowers and gooseberries are in season at the same time and are true partners. Elderflower syrup is a great way to add sweetness to this tart fruit – in a fool, pie or crumble, for example. It's amazing that such a humble and underused edible flower has so many possibilities in the kitchen.

ELDERFLOWER SYRUP *makes about 4 litres*

This is a great standby for many desserts, ice creams and drinks. You can make it as strong as you like – just add more elderflowers to the infusion for a more intense flavour. If you want to make a syrup that's going to keep (like this one), then you will need to put in a fair amount of sugar to preserve it. Once made, simply dilute with fizzy or still water for a refreshing cordial, or try a splash in a glass of Champagne or sparkling wine for an aperitif.

1 carrier bag of elderflowers (about 800g–1 kg, or 20 or so heads)

1kg unrefined or granulated sugar

2 lemons, halved

4 litres water

Remove any leaves and stems from the elderflowers and shake out any insects.

Place the elderflowers in a non-reactive pan with the sugar, squeeze in the lemon juice and add the spent lemon halves to the pan. Pour in the water, bring to the boil, then lower the heat and simmer for just a minute. Remove from the heat, cover and leave to infuse for 24 hours, stirring every so often.

The following day, strain the syrup through a muslin-lined sieve and pour into sterilised bottles. If you wish to keep it longer than a few days, then immerse the filled bottles in a pan of water, bring to the boil and simmer gently for 15 minutes, then leave to cool in the water. Seal the bottles and store in a cool, dark cupboard.

ELDERFLOWER ICE CREAM *makes about 750ml*

Rich and creamy, with a subtle fragrance, this is the perfect ice cream to serve with summer berries and fruit jellies. It is best eaten on the day it is made, though it can be kept in the freezer for a day or two.

300ml creamy milk, such as Guernsey or Jersey

6 egg yolks

100g caster sugar

300ml Jersey cream or clotted cream (or a mixture)

200ml elderflower syrup, or more to taste

Pour the milk into a saucepan and bring to the boil, then remove from the heat.

Whisk the egg yolks and sugar together in a bowl, then pour on the milk, whisking as you do so. Return to the pan and place over a low heat. Cook, stirring constantly, using a whisk, for about 5 minutes until the custard has thickened lightly, but don't let it boil.

Pour the custard into a bowl and whisk in the cream and elderflower syrup. Leave to cool, then churn in an ice-cream machine until thickened. Scoop into glass bowls and serve, with summer berries if you like.

GOOSEBERRY AND ELDERFLOWER
MERINGUE PIE *serves 4*

Some people find the sourness of gooseberries a bit off-putting, but they make really great desserts. With the exception of the red dessert variety, these berries need to be cooked with sugar. The elderflower gives them a complementary summery fragrance.

FOR THE PASTRY

2 medium egg yolks

225g unsalted butter, softened

1 tablespoon caster sugar

275g plain flour, plus extra for dusting

melted butter for brushing

FOR THE FILLING

200g gooseberries

60ml elderflower syrup (see page 100)

60g caster sugar

FOR THE MERINGUE

2 egg whites

40g caster sugar

To make the pastry, beat the egg yolks and butter together in a bowl until evenly blended, then beat in the sugar. Stir in the flour and knead together until well mixed. Wrap the pastry in cling film, flatten and leave to rest in the fridge for an hour before use.

Meanwhile, put the gooseberries, elderflower syrup and sugar in a pan over a medium heat. Cook, stirring every so often, for 5–6 minutes until the gooseberries have softened and the liquid has evaporated. Remove from the heat, cover with a lid or cling film and set aside.

Preheat the oven to 190°C/gas 5. Lightly brush 4 individual flan tins, 8–10cm in diameter and 3cm deep, with melted butter (or one large 20–23cm flan tin, about 4cm deep). Roll out the pastry on a lightly floured surface to a 3mm thickness. Cut out 4 discs (or one big one), large enough to line the flan tin(s).

Line the tin(s) with the pastry, trimming away the excess just above the rims. This pastry is quite delicate but forgiving, so if it starts to break just patch it up, moulding the pastry back together with your fingers. Crimp the edge for a neat finish, by pinching it between your thumb and forefinger all the way round. Leave to rest in the fridge for 1 hour.

Line the pastry case(s) with greaseproof paper discs, fill with baking beans and bake blind for 10–15 minutes until the pastry is lightly golden. Rest for 5 minutes, then remove the beans and paper. Turn the oven setting up to 200°C/gas 6.

Place the egg whites in a clean, dry bowl, making sure it is free from any trace of grease. Whisk, using an electric whisk, until stiff. Add half of the sugar and whisk for 2–3 minutes until the mixture is really stiff, then add the rest of the sugar and continue whisking until the meringue is very stiff and shiny.

To assemble, spoon the gooseberries into the tart case(s), then either pipe or spoon the meringue on top to cover completely. Place on a baking tray and bake in the oven for 3–5 minutes until the meringue just starts to colour. Serve hot or warm.

GOOSEBERRY AND ELDERFLOWER FOOL

This gooseberry compote pie filling can be used to make a creamy fool. Prepare as above and leave to cool.

In a large bowl, mix together 75ml white wine, 20ml elderflower syrup, the juice of ½ lemon and 40g caster sugar. Add 250ml double cream and whip the mixture slowly with an electric whisk until thick. Fold three-quarters of the gooseberry compote into the cream mixture, spoon into glasses or a serving dish and chill for 1–2 hours. Serve topped with the rest of the compote.

July

SALADS AND HERBS *from the* garden, *freshly podded* PEAS AND BEANS, *succulent* Dorset CRAB *and* fragrant STRAWBERRIES... *the true tastes of a British summer*

OTHER INGREDIENTS NOT TO BE MISSED

Salmon   Sea trout   Lobster   Crayfish   Sand eels   Smelts   Samphire   Rock samphire   Sea beet   Sea kale

Scottish girolles   Puffball   Marrows   Courgettes   Wild fennel   Tomatoes   Elderflowers   Blackcurrants

Strawberries   Raspberries   Wild strawberries   Dorset blueberries   Cherries   Red and white currants

July is the height of summer for homegrown produce. There are so many amazing ingredients around now that shopping for dinner is effortless. Great British produce like peas, beans and summer berries are abundant, so don't miss out. Less is certainly more with these foods and you won't need complicated recipes to get the best out of them.

If you're throwing a party then it's hard to beat a simple bowl of mixed summer berries for dessert, served with some thick Jersey cream or homemade ice cream of course.

There are endless other ways to serve berries, jellies being one of my favourites. The great thing with a jelly is that it really captures the flavours of the season. Also, it will keep for a few days so you can get ahead if you're planning a dinner party. What you flavour your jelly with is up to you – it can be as simple as homemade elderflower syrup or as decadent as Champagne. While I was travelling last year, I stumbled across some individual baba (savarin) moulds, which are perfect for serving all kinds of jellies – and you can rest a ball of ice cream in the centre so it doesn't slide all over the plate. It might not be what they were designed for, but these moulds have a new role in my kitchen.

Likewise, beans and peas are true tastes of summer. Apart from their natural ability to accompany both fish and meat, they are perfect, individually or together, in summery salads. At the start of a meal, I quite like to have a bowl of fresh, young peas in their pods on the table to pop and snack on while having drinks – it gives a real sense of the time of year.

And on the subject of salads, you may notice that many of mine consist of unusual-looking salad leaves that you rarely see in the shops. That's because I grow around 90 per cent of my salad leaves for home use. I'll even try to utilise weeds in the garden, like chickweed, bitter cress and nasturtium leaves, to liven up the salad bowl. You can, of course, substitute other leaves, but if you have a garden, why not have a go? There are plenty of seeds available these days through garden centres and over the internet. You'll find them easy to grow and maintain.

One of my big midsummer favourites is crab, which I've been fond of for as long as I can remember. The closest most kids are willing to come to fresh crab is fishing them out of rock pools, but I ate them regularly as a child. Local fisherman would leave them in the porch, along with the occasional lobster if we were lucky. When I left school, before catering college, I worked in The Bridport Arms, the local pub on the beach in West Bay. It was the waitresses' job to prise out the meat from the crabs for salads and sandwiches. After lunch they would get dressed up in protective black bin liners, arm themselves with a hammer and teaspoon and sit around the table to tackle big pots of freshly cooked crabs. The bones and shells went straight into the bins and out with the rubbish, which seems ridiculous to me now. At least, they should be destined for the stockpot – they hold too much flavour to waste.

As a kid, I also used to catch spider crabs (like the one in the photo above) in my prawn drop net, but we were taught to kill them and throw them back. In those days, spider crabs were so prolific they plagued the fishermen's lobster pots. Now, of course, I value their meat, but I have a hunch that it will be some time yet before it really catches on in this country.

July also sees the start of the Scottish girolle season. These are the plump bright yellow mushrooms that are sometimes called golden chanterelles. It's great to have such a colourful mushroom at this time of the year that slots nicely into summery recipes. English chanterelles, which appear later in the year, have a hollow yellow stem and brown cap.

Another little delicacy that I often cook in July is rook. This might not be a regular item on restaurant menus, but young rooks do need to be culled. Tasting rather like pigeon, they are delicious cooked just pink and served in a salad or on a piece of toast, spread with coarsely chopped livers.

Salads and herbs

A good simple salad picked straight from the garden is so satisfying. To grow your own salads and herbs, you don't need a huge area – pots and old cut-down wine barrels work well in a limited space. Just make sure you give the plants plenty of water and a good feed (such as dried chicken manure pellets) – and cut them regularly to encourage new growth. In addition to herbs, I generally grow at least six salad leaf varieties each year, usually experimenting with a couple of new ones. I also keep a back up of seed packets in case I need to do an emergency planting. The following are my favourites to grow.

BABY GEM AND COS LETTUCE: These are essential to add a bit of crunch to salads.

SILVER SORREL: A round-leaved sorrel with a robust leaf and a tangy lemony flavour.

WILD AND STANDARD ROCKET: I like to grow both, as they are sufficiently different. The smaller-leaved wild variety has a stronger, more peppery flavour. You can keep cutting rocket all year round – it will keep growing back with a more lively flavour each time.

SALADAISI: A bit like French mesclun, this is a collection of mixed leaves, including Cos, rocket, chives, chervil and others. If you can't find this particular variety, you'll no doubt come across similar leaf mixes, which can be continually cut once they reach a certain height – usually around 10–12cm. I always have a row in the garden.

AMERICAN LAND CRESS: This has a similar peppery nature to rocket, with a rounder leaf.

PURSLANE: A lovely salad leaf, this has small fibrous leaves attached to a tender red stem.

NASTURTIUM: Both the leaves and flowers of this decorative plant can be tossed into a salad.

BULL'S BLOOD, RED MUSTARD AND AMARANTH: These are great colourful salad leaves, as is oak leaf, which is sometimes sold as red salad bowl lettuce.

I also encourage weeds like bittercress, penywort and chickweed, which most gardeners would toss into the compost or spray with weedkiller. They all have great individual flavours, which will make your salads stand out from those supermarket pre-packed leaves.

Soft herbs like chives, chervil, tarragon, flat leaf parsley can be treated as salad leaves, lending fragrance and flavour to your salads.

Dressings

Dressings are crucial to a good salad and I always try to keep a good selection of oils and vinegars in my larder. Let's face it, if you're going to make a bespoke salad from your garden then the dressing has got to live up to – and complement – the leaves. I'll always have extra virgin rapeseed oil, plus several olive oils, walnut and hazelnut oils, and a mild vegetable oil at hand to whisk into good quality vinegars, such as sherry, cider, aged red wine, Cabernet Sauvignon and Chardonnay. It becomes a bit like the wine room where you can just walk in and knock up a dressing to suit your mood.

As for the choice of dressing, it really depends what you are serving the salad with. If it's a side salad to go with meat or fish dishes, a simple tarragon vinaigrette is a good choice. If your salad is more centre stage, then consider a more robust option, like the blue cheese dressing; this works best with leaves like chicory, Cos or Little Gem.

TARRAGON DRESSING
makes about 100ml

- 1 tablespoon cider vinegar
- 1 teaspoon English mustard (Tewksbury or Norfolk)
- 1 garlic clove, peeled
- a few sprigs of tarragon
- 2 tablespoons virgin rapeseed oil
- 3 tablespoons vegetable or corn oil
- salt and freshly ground black pepper

Put all the ingredients into a clean bottle or jar. Shake well and leave to infuse for at least an hour, preferably overnight, at room temperature. Strain the dressing before tossing with your salad.

BLUE CHEESE DRESSING
makes about 230ml

- 2 tablespoons cider vinegar
- 1 teaspoon English mustard (ideally Suffolk or Tewksbury)
- 50g blue cheese, such as Cornish, Lanark or Stilton
- 120ml vegetable oil
- 30ml water
- salt and freshly ground black pepper

Whiz the cider vinegar, mustard, blue cheese, oil and water in a blender until smooth and season with salt and pepper to taste.

FARMHOUSE SALAD WITH SCOTCH DUCK'S EGG *serves 4*

This main course salad makes a great family meal and you can vary the ingredients as you like. The last time I prepared it I happen to have made the stargazy pie (on page 97) the day before, so I added the rabbit fillets that were left. If you can't find the sausagemeat, just buy some good quality Cumberland sausages and remove the skins.

- 80–100g piece of smoked streaky bacon (or lardons)
- 180–200g good quality black pudding, skinned
- 2 thick slices of bread
- 4 duck's eggs
- 200g good quality Cumberland sausagemeat
- 1 tablespoon plain flour
- 1 egg, beaten
- 40–50g fresh white breadcrumbs
- vegetable oil for deep-frying
- 2–3 tablespoons vegetable or corn oil
- 4 rabbit saddle fillets (optional)
- a knob of butter
- 2 handfuls of small salad and herb leaves (about 80–90g)
- 100ml tarragon dressing (see above)
- salt and freshly ground black pepper

Cut the bacon, black pudding and bread roughly into 1cm chunks and set aside.

Lower the eggs into a pan of simmering water and cook for 3–4 minutes to soft-boil them, then remove and refresh in cold water. Once cool, carefully peel the eggs, keeping them intact. Divide the sausagemeat into 4 balls and flatten them into patties. Wrap each patty around an egg, moulding it to cover evenly with your hands.

Have three shallow containers ready, one containing the flour, one with the egg and the third with the breadcrumbs. One at a time, coat the eggs with the flour first, shaking off any excess, then put through the beaten egg and finally into the breadcrumbs, turning them to coat all over and re-moulding as necessary.

Heat a 6cm depth of oil in a deep-fat fryer or other suitable large, deep, heavy-based pan to 140–150°C.

Deep-fry the eggs for 3–4 minutes, turning occasionally to colour evenly. Remove and drain on kitchen paper.

Heat 1 tablespoon oil in a frying pan. Add the bacon, black pudding and rabbit fillets if using. Cook, stirring, for 2–3 minutes until lightly coloured, then remove with a slotted spoon and keep warm. Heat the rest of the oil in the pan, then add the bread cubes with the butter and fry until crisp and golden; remove and drain.

To serve, dress the leaves with some of the dressing, season and arrange in wide bowls or on plates. Cut each rabbit fillet, if using, into 4 or 5 slices then scatter over the salad leaves with the fried bread, bacon and black pudding. Cut the Scotch eggs in half and arrange on the salad. Drizzle over the rest of the dressing and serve.

HAM HOCK AND PEA SALAD *serves* 4

If you're a keen gardener, you may or may not know that pea shoots or tendrils are perfect for summery salads. Mangetout and bean shoots can be used in the same way – you can even plant them just for their young shoots and keep cutting them through the summer as they grow back.

Often the most successful salads are those where you simply throw one or two tasty ingredients into the salad bowl – freshly cooked ham tossed with tender peas and shoots makes a great starter, lunch or light main dish, for example. If you haven't got pea shoots in the garden, try to source them in farmers' markets or Chinese food stores.

A ham hock or knuckle has a fantastic flavour and goes a long way. Once cooked, you have a great stock base for a soup. Simmer peas and/or broad beans in it and blend to make a smooth soup, or prepare a summery minestrone flaking some of the off-cuts of the hock back in.

TO COOK THE HAM HOCK
1 ham hock (smoked or unsmoked), about 1kg or so, soaked overnight in cold water

1 onion, peeled and quartered

1 leek, halved lengthways and washed

10 black peppercorns

1 bay leaf

a few sprigs of thyme

3 juniper berries

FOR THE SALAD
120–150g freshly podded peas

salt and freshly ground black pepper

1–2 teaspoons granulated sugar

a few good knobs of butter

a little vegetable oil (optional)

2 handfuls of pea shoots

100ml tarragon dressing (see page 110)

Drain the ham hock, rinse and place in a large cooking pot with the flavouring ingredients. Add enough cold water to cover generously and bring to the boil. Skim off any scum from the surface and simmer, covered, for 2–2½ hours or until the ham is tender.

Leave the ham hock to cool in the liquid (unless you're in a hurry, in which case remove it to a board to cool more quickly).

Bring enough water to the boil in a pan to cook the peas. Add salt, the sugar and butter, then tip in the peas. Simmer for 3–5 minutes or until tender. Drain well.

Remove enough of the ham from the hock for the salad and break it into flakes with your fingers. (You could also dice some of the rind and fry it in a little hot oil to crisp up.)

Toss the pea shoots, peas and the ham in the dressing and arrange on plates or in shallow bowls to serve.

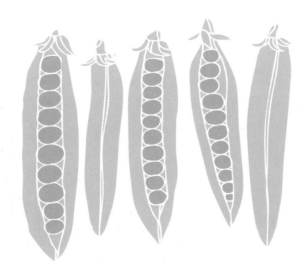

Summer peas and beans

As we can easily buy green beans and peas all year round, we are inclined to forget that we have our very own – albeit short – season for them. Like all other fruit and veg, I prefer to wait and enjoy our own produce, though I do keep a bag of frozen peas in my freezer for the occasional emergency risotto.

Apart from the traditional ways of serving summer beans and peas as a hot accompaniment, they offer scope for a variety of interesting dishes. Young peas and beans are great just tossed into a salad with some tasty green leaves and maybe some goat's cheese. I also use their shoots or tendrils to add texture and character to salads.

Or try making a sauce to accompany fish as I do, by gently cooking some bacon and shallots, then adding peas and simmering in a little fish stock and cream. Also, blended peas and beans make great summer dips – with some good olive oil, lemon juice and seasoning added – rather like fresh houmous.

CHILLED PEA AND LOVAGE SOUP *serves* 4

Pea and mint is of course a classic combination and may be the obvious choice for a soup, but lovage also complements peas really well. Like mint, it is very fragrant and has a special flavour but it is an underused herb, probably because of its potency. Certainly, lovage must be added with caution or it will overpower other flavours. I always have some in the garden because it's great walking out the back door and grabbing a few leaves of something that's so hard to find in the shops.

    1 tablespoon vegetable or corn oil
    1 leek (both green and white parts),
    trimmed, roughly chopped and washed
    1.2 litres vegetable stock
    salt and freshly ground black pepper
    450g freshly podded peas (or frozen ones
    will do)
    10–12 lovage leaves

Heat the oil in a pan, add the leek and cook gently for 3–4 minutes, stirring occasionally until soft. Add the stock, season and simmer gently for 10–12 minutes.

Tip in the peas and simmer for another 5 minutes or until tender (frozen peas will only need a couple minutes once they come back to a simmer). Add the lovage and immediately take off the heat.

Whiz the mixture in a blender until smooth, then taste. Adjust the seasoning and blend in some more lovage if you think the soup needs it. Pass through a sieve if you wish (some blenders do a better job than others). Serve hot or cold.

LAMB SWEETBREADS WITH PEAS *serves* 4

I first tasted this combination at Alastair Little's restaurant in Soho some 17 years ago and remember how good it was. Sweetbreads are the thymus glands of the animal – found in the throat and near the heart, or at least that's what they usually are. At the Abergavenny Food Festival a couple of years ago, I ordered lamb sweetbreads for a demonstration but was sent lamb's testicles instead, as this is what they are called in that part of the world. I cooked them anyway and they went down a storm. Sweetbreads are hard to find in supermarkets, and you may need to order them from your butcher in advance. Choose nice, plump lamb sweetbreads if possible, otherwise don't worry.

    500g lamb's sweetbreads
    salt and freshly ground black pepper
    2 knobs of butter
    3 shallots, peeled and finely chopped
    100ml white wine
    200ml light chicken stock (or ½ good
    stock cube dissolved in this amount of
    boiling water)
    300g freshly podded peas
    200ml double cream
    1–2 tablespoons rapeseed or vegetable oil
    1 tablespoon chopped parsley

Soak the sweetbreads in cold water for about 1 hour, then drain and put them into a pan. Cover with cold water and add 2 teaspoons salt. Bring to the boil and simmer for 2 minutes, then drain in a colander and refresh under the cold tap for a minute to cool them down. Remove the outer membrane and any sinew from the sweetbreads and put them to one side.

Heat a knob of butter in a pan and gently cook the shallots for 2–3 minutes until soft. Add the white wine and chicken stock and boil until almost totally reduced. Meanwhile, add the peas to a pan of boiling salted water and simmer for 3–4 minutes until almost tender; drain.

Add the cream to the shallots and simmer until it has reduced by a third. Add the peas, season with salt and pepper and simmer for another 2 minutes.

Meanwhile, heat the oil in a non-stick (or faithful) frying pan. Season the sweetbreads and fry them over a high heat until they begin to colour. Add a little butter and continue to cook until crisp. Remove from the pan and drain on kitchen paper. Add the sweetbreads to the peas with the parsley and simmer for a couple of minutes. Serve at once, with new potatoes if you like.

SALT BEEF AND GREEN BEAN SALAD

serves 4

Whenever I visit Paris, a lunch in Chez Georges in rue du Mail is a must. It's a delightful little old brasserie with a classic and extremely simple menu. Order ox cheek salad and you'll get a bowl of sliced salted ox cheek (enough to feed at least four) in a good vinaigrette with shallots and skinny French beans, along with an empty plate. You just help yourself. No fuss, no pretence ... and bloody good.

Salted ox cheeks are tricky to get unless you order them specially, but if you fancy trying to re-create this dish, you can use salted brisket as a substitute. It has layers of fat running through it, which keeps the meat meltingly tender. Silverside is too lean.

The elements for this dish can be prepared well ahead, if you've got people for lunch or dinner. You'll need to start the day before anyway, as the beef needs to be soaked overnight.

700–800g salted beef brisket or salted ox cheeks, soaked overnight in cold water

2 onions, peeled and quartered

2 carrots, peeled and trimmed

10 black peppercorns

4 garlic cloves, peeled

a few sprigs of thyme

100g French beans, trimmed

salt and freshly ground black pepper

2 large shallots, peeled and finely chopped

FOR THE VINAIGRETTE

1½ tablespoons good quality tarragon vinegar

2 teaspoons Dijon mustard

1 garlic clove, peeled

3 tablespoons olive oil

3 tablespoons vegetable or corn oil

First make the vinaigrette. Put all the ingredients into a clean bottle or screw-topped jar and season with salt and pepper. Shake it and leave to infuse overnight at room temperature.

Rinse the salt beef and put it into a saucepan with the onions, carrots, peppercorns, garlic and thyme sprigs. Cover well with water, bring to the boil and skim off the scum from the surface, then simmer, covered, for about 2 hours, topping up the water if necessary. It's difficult to put an exact cooking time on cuts of meat like this, so check it after 2 hours and if it's not tender cook for another half an hour or so. Leave to cool in the liquid, but don't refrigerate.

Cook the French beans in boiling salted water for 3–4 minutes until tender, then drain well.

Remove the beef from the cooking liquid and carve into 5mm thick slices, breaking these up into bite-sized pieces. Mix the beef with the beans and shallots, season with salt and pepper to taste and dress well with the vinaigrette to serve.

Crab

I strongly recommend buying live crab and cooking and dressing it yourself, unless you have a very trustworthy fishmonger. I often find that precooked and dressed crab feels like it's been hanging around a bit too long, probably due to my upbringing by the sea.

There are two recommended 'humane' ways of preparing your crab ready for cooking. The first is to turn your live crab on its back and drive an awl or sturdy skewer between the eyes, then lift the tail flap and drive the skewer through the centre of the body. The legs will go limp once its dead. The other way is to put the crab in the freezer, to send it to sleep.

TO COOK THE CRAB: Bring a pan of heavily salted water to the boil (about 1 tablespoon salt per litre). Plunge the crab in, bring back to the boil and simmer for about 15 minutes for the first 500g, then an extra 5–6 minutes for every additional 500g. Remove from the water and leave to cool.

TO GET THE MEAT OUT OF THE CRAB: Twist the legs and claws off, then crack them open with a hammer or similar implement and remove the white meat with a lobster pick or teaspoon. Now turn the crab on its back and twist off the pointed flap. Push the tip of a table knife between the main shell and the body section to which the legs were attached. Twist the blade to separate the two, then push the body up and remove from the outer shell. Scoop out the brown meat from the main shell and put to one side. From the other section, remove the dead man's fingers (these are the feather-like, grey gills attached to the body) and discard. Split the body in half with a heavy knife and then split each half in half again. Now you need to be patient and pick out the white meat from the little cavities in the body using a lobster pick or a teaspoon. This centre shell is very brittle, but you will get a fair bit of meat from it if you are careful. Go through the white and brown meat separately to make sure there are no residual bits of shell.

TO DRESS THE CRAB: Or serve it the traditional way back in the shell, you'll need to prepare the main shell. Look for the definite line surrounding the open part and push the edge in gently with your fingers. It will break along the line, leaving a neat cavity. Wash the shell under warm water, give it a light scrub and dry with a kitchen cloth.

Mix up the brown meat a little, adding a little mayonnaise if you wish, then spoon into the centre of the shell, placing the white meat on either side. Alternatively, just serve a good spoonful of each on a plate, with a wedge of lemon and brown bread and butter.

Don't discard the shells, claws, etc. – they are full of flavour. Instead use them to make a stock, soup (see page 123) or shellfish-infused oil (see page 123).

CRAB SALAD *serves 4 as a starter*

A salad is an easy option if you're not going to dress your crab traditionally or turn it into a sandwich. All you need is some tasty seasonal leaves and perhaps a chopped tomato or two, or, if it's early summer, a few blanched asparagus tips maybe.

I tend to use just the leaves from my garden during the summer – peppery leaves like nasturtium and land cress, plus flat leaf parsley, chervil and some bitter cress and chickweed. Sometimes I add other herbs like chives and perhaps a spring onion.

You could also use shellfish oil (see page 123) in the dressing to enhance the flavour.

about 200–250g white crab meat

50–60g brown crab meat

1 tablespoon mayonnaise (see below)

salt and freshly ground black pepper

squeeze of lemon juice, to taste

2 handfuls of small salad leaves

2 tomatoes, skinned, deseeded and finely chopped

1 tablespoon snipped chives

FOR THE DRESSING

1 tablespoon cider vinegar

2 teaspoons brown crab meat (optional)

2 tablespoons rapeseed oil

2 tablespoons vegetable or corn oil

a few sprigs of tarragon

First make the dressing. Whisk all of the ingredients together, seasoning to taste and adding a teaspoonful of the brown crab meat if you like. (It binds the ingredients together, rather like mustard does in a vinaigrette, and adds richness.)

For the salad, fork through the white crab meat, checking for any fragments of shell, and set aside. Mix the brown meat with the mayonnaise and season to taste with salt and pepper, adding a squeeze of lemon.

Arrange the salad leaves on serving plates and scatter the chopped tomatoes over. Remove the tarragon from the dressing, then drizzle over the salad leaves. Arrange the white crab on the leaves and put a spoonful of the brown crab mix in the centre. Scatter the snipped chives over to serve.

MAYONNAISE *makes about 350ml*

Good mayonnaise is essential for seafood. It's not that tricky to make and it will keep in the fridge for a couple of weeks. If you're going to the trouble of cooking and picking the meat out of a crab, cheap shop-bought mayonnaise really doesn't do it justice.

2 egg yolks (at room temperature)

2 teaspoons good quality cider or white wine vinegar

1 teaspoon English mustard

2 teaspoons Dijon mustard

salt and freshly ground black pepper

100ml olive oil

200ml vegetable oil

squeeze of lemon juice, to taste

Use a glass or stainless steel bowl (not an aluminium one as this will cause the mayonnaise to discolour). Put the egg yolks, vinegar, mustards, ½ teaspoon salt and a little pepper into the bowl and place on a damp cloth to stop it slipping. Mix well with a whisk.

Combine the oils, then gradually trickle onto the egg yolk mixture, whisking continuously. If the mayonnaise starts to get too thick, add a few drops of water and continue whisking in the oil. When the oil is all incorporated, taste, adjust the seasoning if necessary and add a little lemon juice to taste.

If not using immediately, store in a sealed jar in the fridge.

SPIDER CRAB ON TOAST *serves 4 as a snack*

Spider crab is one of those relatively undiscovered seafood pleasures... well at least in the UK. It can be prepared and eaten in exactly the same way as a standard brown crab, but don't expect to get quite as much white meat out of it. You'll also need to work a little harder at getting that white meat out of the body crevices.

Fresh crab meat on toast – either from a spider crab or a regular brown crab – makes a delicious snack, or you can serve it as a starter for a dinner party with, perhaps, a small herb salad on the side. I would recommend using a sourdough bread here to give a nice crisp, full-flavoured base for the crab.

> 2 spider crabs, each about 600g, or 1 crab, 1kg or more, white and brown meat picked
>
> salt and freshly ground white pepper
>
> 1–2 tablespoons mayonnaise (see page 119)
>
> squeeze of lemon juice, to taste
>
> 4 slices of sourdough bread, about 1cm thick
>
> softened butter for spreading

Season the white and brown crab separately and mix the brown meat with a little mayonnaise and lemon juice, or just mix the whole lot together if you like.

Toast the bread on both sides and butter one side. If you've kept the brown and white meat separate, spread the brown on first and the white on top, or if it's mixed simply spoon on top of the toasts. Serve at once.

CRAB SANDWICH *serves 4*

You can't beat a good crab sandwich. I've had some pretty appalling ones in the past, so now I won't order one unless I know the establishment. I suppose I was spoilt in my childhood – crab straight off the boat, into the pot, into a sandwich and eaten within 24 hours.

For a good crab sandwich, you need very fresh crab – and plenty of white claw meat in particular. Good wholemeal bread and homemade mayonnaise are also essential. I've known breadcrumbs to be mixed into the brown meat along with the mayo. That's understandable if the meat is wet, but otherwise I wouldn't advocate this as it will weaken the flavour.

> 2 crabs, each about 500–600g, or 1 crab, about 1kg, white and brown meat picked
>
> 2–3 tablespoons mayonnaise (see page 119)
>
> salt and freshly ground white pepper
>
> squeeze of lemon juice, to taste (optional)
>
> 8 slices of wholemeal bread, ½cm thick
>
> softened butter for spreading
>
> lemon wedges, to serve

Check the crab meat for any tiny fragments of shell and keep the brown and white meat separate.

Put the brown crab meat into a bowl and mix with 1–2 tablespoons of the mayonnaise. Season with salt and pepper to taste and add a little lemon juice if you wish. Butter the bread and spread a couple of tablespoonfuls of the brown meat mix onto half of the slices.

Spread a little mayonnaise on the other slices of bread. Lightly season the white meat and pile it on to these slices. Ideally, you want to use about double the quantity of white meat to brown meat, although it depends on your taste and how much brown meat you've managed to get out of your crab(s).

Sandwich the slices together. Cut in half or into quarters and serve with lemon wedges, for squeezing.

Any leftover crab can be mixed together and spread onto hot buttered toast.

CRAB SOUP *serves 4–6*

Crab isn't cheap to buy, so it really makes sense to get full value from it. Once you've enjoyed your crab feast, or made a sandwich or salad, you can crush the shells and freeze them for later use, or make this soup straight away if you have time and freeze it.

500–700g crab shells, broken into
small pieces

1 tablespoon vegetable oil

1 small onion, peeled and roughly chopped

1 small leek, rinsed, trimmed, roughly
chopped and washed

1 small fennel bulb, trimmed and roughly
chopped

4 garlic cloves, peeled and chopped

½ teaspoon fennel seeds

a few sprigs of thyme

1 bay leaf

a few good knobs of butter

2 tablespoons tomato purée

3 tablespoons plain flour

a glass of white wine

2 litres fish stock (or 2 good stock cubes
dissolved in this amount of boiling water)

salt and freshly ground white pepper

3–4 tablespoons double cream

about 100g white crab meat (optional)

Put the shells into a strong carrier bag and smash them up with a steak hammer or rolling pin (the bag will stop the shells flying around all over your kitchen worktop).

Heat the oil in a large heavy-based saucepan and fry the crab shells over a high heat for about 5 minutes, stirring every so often until they begin to colour. Add the onion, leek, fennel, garlic, fennel seeds, thyme and bay leaf, and continue cooking for another 5 minutes or so until the vegetables begin to colour.

Stir in the butter, followed by the tomato purée and flour. Cook, stirring, over a low heat for a minute or so. Add the white wine, then slowly add the fish stock, stirring to avoid any lumps. Bring to the boil, season with salt and pepper, and simmer gently for about 1 hour.

Strain the soup, shells and all, through a colander set over a bowl, stirring the shells so that any small pieces go into the liquid. Pick out about a third of the softer white body shells in the sieve (not the hard claws or main shell). Add these to the strained liquor and discard the rest of the sieve contents. Tip the liquor and reserved shells into a strong blender or food processor and whiz until smooth, then strain through a fine sieve into a clean pan.

Taste the soup and adjust the seasoning as necessary, then bring to the boil. Stir in the cream, check the seasoning again and serve. If you like, stir a spoonful of flaked white crab meat into each portion before serving.

VARIATION You can also convert this soup into a delicious crab sauce to serve with fish dishes, or even chicken. Once you've puréed it, add about 300ml double cream and simmer until it has thickened to the required consistency, then strain through a fine sieve.

SHELLFISH-INFUSED OIL *makes 1 litre*

This is another good way to get the best out of tasty crab, lobster or crayfish carcasses, or prawn shells. Keep it in the fridge and use for dressing salads or fish.

200g crab (or other crustacea) shells

1 litre oil (ideally a mixture of rapeseed
and vegetable or corn oil)

1 teaspoon fennel seeds

12 black peppercorns

a small pinch of saffron strands

a good pinch of sea salt

a few sprigs of thyme

Put the shells into a large saucepan and add all the other ingredients. Slowly bring to a simmer. Continue to simmer very gently over the lowest possible heat for about 15 minutes, to infuse the oil with the flavours from the shells and aromatics.

Remove the pan from the heat and set aside to infuse for 2–3 hours.

Strain the infused oil through a muslin-lined sieve and store in sterilised bottles in the fridge. Once opened, use within 2–3 weeks.

Strawberries

Strawberries have come to symbolise summer and everything about it. Wimbledon wouldn't be the same without vendors charging extortionate prices for those little tubs of them and that summer fruit salad would be naked and skinny without them. Simple and obvious perhaps, but is there really a better dessert than fragrant, ripe strawberries with thick cream and caster sugar? That is as long as they are in season, of course. It's beyond me why people buy strawberries that have done a good few air miles in December when it's freezing cold outside. They never fail to disappoint.

My favourite variety is the Alpine strawberry or fraises de bois. They do grow wild in abundance in this country if you know where to find them, and there are a few growers producing them in Kent. They are tiny, about the size of a fingernail, with an intense flavour. There is even a white variety, which I've chosen to use in my trifle.

In the height of summer, I'll serve strawberries at least a couple of times a week. They also make great drinks for kids and adults. Freeze them when they're cheap and just pop them frozen into the blender with milk or yoghurt to make a great milkshake or smoothie. I'm not keen on cooking strawberries, but they are lovely preserved in eau de vie – perfect with ice cream for a lively, simple pudding.

STRAWBERRY SUNDAE *serves* 4

Fruit sundaes and knickerbocker glories conjure up memories of traditional British seaside holidays, although you rarely see them on menus these days. You're more likely to come across bought-in ice creams in every flavour under the sun. This seaside classic can be made with whatever fruit is in season at the time, but good quality vanilla ice cream is crucial, homemade or bought.

300–350g strawberries, hulled

about 120ml clotted cream

about 400ml good quality vanilla ice cream (preferably homemade, see page 126)

Whiz about half of the strawberries in a blender until smooth, then strain the purée through a fine sieve to remove the seeds if you wish.

Slice the rest of the strawberries. Put a few strawberry slices in each of four tall glasses and spoon in some of the purée and clotted cream. Pile three small balls of ice cream into the glasses, scattering in more strawberry slices as you do so. Spoon on the rest of the strawberry purée and clotted cream, then top with the remaining strawberry slices to serve.

WILD STRAWBERRY TRIFLE *serves 4*

The trifle I remember as a kid consisted of tinned diced fruits and sherry-soaked sponge under a pile of Bird's custard. Since then I've discovered that trifle is an interesting, versatile dessert that can be adapted to take all sorts of fruits (preferably not tinned). Summer and autumn berries are perfect. Here I've been a bit extravagant and used wild strawberries, but if you can't find any, just use ordinary British strawberries.

A trifle as delicate as this one really doesn't need to be spiked with sherry, as the intense flavour of the strawberries in the jelly should shine through. I've even left out the sponge in this recipe and folded a bit of meringue into the cream topping, but you can put a sponge layer on the bottom if you like.

100–150g wild strawberries (or sliced ordinary strawberries)

FOR THE JELLY
220ml water
150g ripe strawberries
80g caster sugar
6g leaf gelatine (2 sheets)

FOR THE CUSTARD
300ml single cream
½ vanilla pod
5 egg yolks
60g caster sugar
2 teaspoons cornflour

FOR THE TOPPING
250ml double cream
40g caster sugar
50–60g cooked meringue (see page 144)

For the jelly, put the water, strawberries and sugar into a pan. Bring to the boil, then lower the heat and simmer gently for about 8–10 minutes.

Meanwhile, soak the gelatine in a shallow bowl of cold water for a minute or so until soft.

Take the pan off the heat and strain the strawberries through a fine sieve, pushing some of the pulp through. Squeeze out the water from the gelatine, then add to the hot strained syrup and stir until fully dissolved. Leave the jelly to cool, but do not let it set.

Divide a quarter of the wild strawberries among four individual glass serving dishes or scatter them over the bottom of one large glass dish and pour over half of the cooled liquid jelly. Leave in the fridge to set. Repeat with another quarter of the strawberries and the rest of the jelly and leave to set.

Meanwhile, make the custard. Put the single cream into a small saucepan. Split the vanilla pod lengthways, scrape out the seeds with the point of a knife and add to the cream. Slowly bring to the boil, then remove from the heat and leave to infuse for about 10 minutes. In a bowl, mix the egg yolks, sugar and cornflour together.

Take out the vanilla pod and pour the cream onto the egg mixture, mixing well with a whisk. Return to the pan and cook gently over a low heat, stirring constantly with a wooden spoon until the custard thickens; don't let it boil. Remove from the heat and give it a final mix with a whisk. Transfer to a bowl, lay a sheet of cling film on the surface of the custard to prevent it forming a skin and leave to cool for about 30 minutes.

Once the jelly has set, spoon the cooled custard evenly on top, then cover and leave to set in the fridge for half an hour or so.

For the topping, whip the double cream with the sugar in a bowl until fairly firm and put into the fridge until the custard on the trifle has set. Break the meringue into pieces and fold into the cream mixture. Spoon over the custard layer and scatter the rest of the wild strawberries on top of the trifle.

PERRY JELLY WITH SUMMER FRUITS *serves* 4

Whenever Perry is mentioned, it usually provokes the question, what's that? In fact it's the equivalent of cider, but made with pears. I remember the branded version, Babycham as a kid because my grandfather kept those saucer-shaped glasses in the house for special occasions. It might have been a popular drink with the ladies in those days but it probably damaged the reputation of real Perry. Sadly the art of Perry-making hardly exists these days – it's time for a revival, perhaps. Flavouring a jelly with Perry to serve as a dessert is a good way to introduce it or remind people of it. I'd recommend serving it with elderflower ice cream as I did successfully in *Great British Menu*.

500ml Perry

70g caster sugar

4 sheets of leaf gelatine

120g mixed berries (blueberries, raspberries, wild strawberries, etc.)

TO SERVE
elderflower ice cream (see page 101) or vanilla ice cream (see below)

Bring 100ml of the Perry to the boil in a pan. Add the sugar and stir until dissolved.

Meanwhile, soak the gelatine in a shallow bowl of cold water for a minute or so to soften.

Remove the Perry syrup from the heat. Squeeze out the water from the gelatine, then add to the hot Perry and stir until dissolved. Add the rest of Perry, stir well and set aside to cool, but do not let it set.

Divide the berries among four individual jelly moulds or glasses, or scatter them over the base of one large mould. Pour in half of the cooled jelly and place in the fridge for an hour or so to set.

Top up with the rest of the berries and liquid jelly. (Setting the jelly in two phases helps to keep the berries suspended in the jelly so they don't float to the top.) Return to the fridge to set.

To serve, unmould the fruit jellies onto individual plates or a large serving plate as appropriate (unless, of course, you've set them in glasses). Serve the jellies topped with a generous scoop of elderflower or vanilla ice cream if you like.

VANILLA ICE CREAM *makes about* 1 *litre*

Don't even think of making vanilla ice cream on the cheap… you might as well buy it. You'll need lots of egg yolks and cream, plus a nice creamy milk such as gold top, Guernsey or Jersey. Fresh, good quality vanilla pods are essential – not ones that have been lying around for years, drying out and losing their fragrance. You can boost their flavour by adding a little good quality vanilla extract, such as Madagascar Bourbon vanilla extract, but not artificial flavouring.

400ml milk, such as gold top or Guernsey or Jersey

1½ vanilla pods

1½ teaspoons vanilla extract (optional)

6 egg yolks

150g caster sugar

400ml Jersey cream or clotted cream, or a mixture

Pour the milk into a heavy-based saucepan. Split the vanilla pods lengthways, scrape out the seeds with the tip of the knife and add them to the milk; add the empty pods, too. Slowly bring the milk to the boil, then remove from the heat and add the vanilla extract if using.

Whisk the egg yolks and sugar together in a bowl, then gradually pour on the hot milk, whisking well. Return to the pan and cook over a low heat, stirring constantly with a whisk, for about 5 minutes until slightly thickened, but don't let it boil.

Pour the custard into a bowl and whisk in the cream. Leave to cool, then churn in an ice-cream machine until thickened. Scoop into balls to serve.

VARIATIONS Substitute the vanilla with blended soft or poached fruits or coffee, or add chopped up candied ginger halfway through churning.

August

The start of the GAME *season, time to fish for* WILD SALMON *and* SEA TROUT, *homegrown* TOMATOES *in abundance and sweet* Dorset *blueberries*

OTHER INGREDIENTS NOT TO BE MISSED

Sea bass   Sea bream   Plaice   Prawns   Pike   Surf clams   Grouse   Snipe   Wood pigeon

Scottish girolles   Parasol mushrooms   Puffball   Samphire   Sea purslane   Wild sorrel

Wood sorrel   Watercress   Water celery   Borage   Wild orach   Laver   Lovage   Peas and beans   Cucumbers

Samphire   Peppers   Marrows   Elderberries   Damsons   Blackcurrants   Greengages   Gooseberries

Loganberries   Cherries   Victoria plums   Sloes   Green walnuts

August evokes vivid memories. Even now, I can recall the aroma as my grandfather opened the sliding doors of his greenhouses when they were full of tomatoes or chrysanthemums. He was the local expert on 'chrysanths' as he called them and each year he would graft different varieties and enter them in the Chelsea flower show – usually returning with well-earned accolades. His tomato growing was equally prolific, but less inventive. Year in, year out, it was just the one variety – Moneymaker. Supper was often a simple plate of tomatoes with Sarson's malt vinegar, salt and buttered bread. Like the growing there was nothing experimental happening in the kitchen with Grandad's tomatoes. They were what they were – simple, round and full of flavour.

It's worth growing your own tomatoes if you possibly can, as it's not easy to find homegrown produce, with the decline of commercial tomato growing in the UK over the years. No doubt when cheaper Dutch and other foreign imports hit the market, many of our growers were forced out of business.

Thankfully a few of our tomato growers are now experimenting with heritage varieties, which are interesting and full of flavour. Harmony Heritage Tomatoes in Jersey have an incredible set-up, growing more than ten varieties at a time. Kevin Herve, who runs the company, buys boxes of bumblebees from Holland to pollinate his tomatoes naturally. I'm sure there are other small British growers doing much the same and we should encourage them, to get British tomatoes firmly back on the menu.

With our simple food upbringing, game was not on the menu at my Gran's house that often, except for the odd rabbit or hare stew. Now at this time of year I can't wait to tuck into my first grouse of the season. August marks the beginning of our game bird season and the glorious 12ᵀᴴ will be in all game lovers' diaries, so as not to miss out on the first grouse. I've also included the humble pigeon in this chapter, which is often regarded as being at the other end of the spectrum to grouse, but makes very good eating. Pigeons are at their best during July and August when they've been munching on farmers' crops and, of course, this is the obvious time to shoot them. They're also useful target practice before the game season really gets going, as they can fly as fast as most game birds.

This is also the time of year when I like to make one of on my fishing expeditions to Scotland. Of course wild salmon are few and far between, but I've noticed over the past couple of years that the salmon stocks seem to be on the up. This is due to a couple of main factors. Firstly, in the past many of the top salmon rivers suffered because so many salmon got netted out at sea before they could make their journey up river to spawn (and others were caught on their way back). Many of the fishermen responsible for this have been stopped from netting salmon now and their licences bought out by the river authorities.

Secondly, rivers are creating salmon hatcheries that catch small salmon fry and release these wild fish when they are of a size that they can fend for themselves. This has made a difference to stocks because the small fry are particularly vulnerable to predators like cormorants and other large birds, seals, pike and, believe it or not, brown trout. When fishing in Scotland I'd always returned brown trout until the gillie gave me a bollocking and told me they are responsible for eating the salmon eggs.

Sea trout are similarly under threat and populations have declined. It could be argued that you should avoid eating wild salmon and sea trout altogether, but cooking the odd one that you've caught yourself won't do too much damage to the fish stocks… and if you've landed the fish yourself and struggled for half an hour to get it onto the riverbank then it really will taste a hell of a lot better than one from the fishmongers.

When I was growing up in Dorset, I was unaware of the celebrated local blueberries. We put imported blueberries into our shopping baskets right through the year, though they rarely taste of much, forgetting that we have them growing here to enjoy right now. Blueberries are as versatile as any other summer berry and like the other darker berries – tayberries, blackberries and elderberries – their season runs into autumn. If you are a keen forager you can also find wild blueberries, or blaeberries as they are called in certain parts of the country. These are half the size (or less) of a standard blueberry and perfect to toss into a game salad or sauce, or to combine with other berries for a fruity dessert or brunchy pancake.

Grouse and wood pigeon

Apart from kicking off the game season, grouse is a truly delicious bird to roast quite simply, without too many frills. It's a shame to braise it, unless you've been spoilt with an abundance of birds and are bored of roasting it. Try this twist for a change: Make a bread sauce (see page 217) much thicker than normal, set it in the fridge, then slice and pan-fry it (as you would polenta) and serve with a grouse breast and leg on top, as a starter. For a garnish, I add a leafy salad dotted with bacon and parsnip crisps. It's a great way to get the most from an expensive bird, and an ideal choice in the game season if you're serving a fish main course.

I've chosen to put wood pigeon in this month too, as it's generally the best time to eat it. Like grouse, pigeons are plump and flavoursome now, as they'll have been gorging on autumn shoots and berries (when they are not pilfering farmers' crops). They are less expensive than grouse, but can be treated in the same way. Their tender flesh is also great in a salad starter with berries such as blaeberries (tiny wild blueberries) or even redcurrants.

GROUSE ON TOAST WITH DANDELION

serves 4 *as a starter*

If you're a grouse lover, this little starter is a good way to make the deliciously rich meat go just that little bit further. You can, of course, serve other game, like wild duck, teal, widgeon or snipe, in this way. If the grouse giblets have been removed, buy 120g chicken or duck livers to use instead.

2 oven-ready grouse, livers reserved

a few knobs of butter

2 shallots, peeled and finely chopped

1 garlic clove, peeled and crushed

salt and freshly ground black pepper

2 tablespoons sherry

4 slices of white or brown bread, cut 1cm thick, from a small bloomer loaf

handful of dandelion leaves or small other salad leaves, washed

FOR THE DRESSING

1 tablespoon sherry vinegar

3 tablespoons walnut oil

Preheat the oven to 220°C/gas 7. Clean the livers, cut them into even-sized pieces and pat dry with kitchen paper. Heat a good knob of butter in a frying pan and briefly fry the shallots and garlic for a minute or so without colouring. Season the livers and add to them to the pan. Fry over a medium heat for 2–3 minutes, stirring every so often. Stir in the sherry, then remove the pan from the heat.

Rub the breasts of the grouse with butter, season with salt and pepper and place in a roasting pan. Roast in the oven for 10–15 minutes, keeping them nice and pink.

Meanwhile, for the dressing, whisk the sherry vinegar and walnut oil together and season to taste.

Chop the liver mixture by hand or in a food processor, as finely or coarsely as you wish, tasting and seasoning again if necessary. Toast the bread on both sides, then spread with the liver mixture.

Remove the breasts from the grouse, slice and arrange on top of the liver toasts. Shred any leg meat from the birds and mix with the dandelion leaves and dressing. Season and arrange on plates, placing the warm liver toasts in the centre. Serve at once.

CLASSIC ROAST GROUSE *serves* 4

Grouse has a fine flavour that, in my view, is best appreciated if the bird isn't hung for too long. I like to roast it quickly in a hot oven with a knob of butter inside to keep it moist, rather than covered with rashers of bacon that interfere with the flavour of the bird. If you really want bacon, then I suggest you cook it separately. I know it's difficult to change one's eating habits, especially if you've been brought up on game, but that's my theory on the pure grouse eating pleasure.

4 oven-ready young grouse, livers and hearts reserved

salt and freshly ground black pepper

5 knobs of butter, softened

4 sage leaves

2 shallots, peeled and finely chopped

a few knobs of lard

4 slices of white bread, crusts removed

splash of red wine

1 cupful of game or chicken stock, or water

a little cornflour (optional)

bread sauce (see page 217), to serve

Preheat the oven to 220°C/gas 7. Season the grouse inside and out, rub the breasts with butter and put a knob inside each cavity, along with a sage leaf. Roast for 15–20 minutes, for medium rare, basting every so often.

Meanwhile, melt a good knob of butter in a small frying pan and gently cook the shallots without colouring for a few minutes. Season the grouse livers and hearts, add to the pan and cook over a high heat for a couple of minutes. Tip into a small food processor and whiz to a coarse paste, or finely chop by hand.

Melt the lard in a roasting pan on the hob and fry the bread until nicely browned on one side. Remove from the heat, turn the bread over and spread the browned side with the paste; keep hot.

Remove the grouse from the roasting pan, transfer to a warm platter and set aside in a warm place to rest. Place the roasting pan over a medium heat and pour in the wine and stock or water, stirring with a wooden spoon to deglaze and scrape up the sediment. Let bubble for a minute or so. If you prefer a thicker gravy, mix a little cornflour with a tablespoonful of water, add to the pan and simmer, stirring, for another minute.

Serve the grouse, on or off the bone, with the croûtes, pan gravy, bread sauce and other accompaniments of your choice.

WOOD PIGEON, SILVER SORREL AND COBNUT SALAD *serves 4 as a starter*

My single silver sorrel plant, which I introduced into my salad patch a couple of years ago, has gone mad, spreading and re-rooting itself quicker than I can eat it. Perhaps it's just as well, as it has become one of my favourite salad leaves. A small, almost heart-shaped, robust leaf, it has a unique tangy flavour. If you can't find cobnuts, which are really particular to Kent, then use walnuts or hazelnuts instead.

2 oven-ready wood pigeons
salt and freshly ground black pepper
a couple of thyme sprigs
a few knobs of butter
25–30 cobnuts, shelled
1 teaspoon sea salt
½ tablespoon rapeseed oil
2 thick slices of smoked streaky bacon, cut into ½cm dice
a couple of handfuls of silver sorrel or other small salad leaves
FOR THE DRESSING
1 tablespoon cider vinegar
1 teaspoon mustard
4 tablespoons rapeseed oil

Preheat the oven to 220°C/gas 7. Season the pigeons inside and out and put a thyme sprig inside each cavity with a knob of butter. Rub the breasts with butter. Roast for 10–12 minutes, keeping the meat nice and pink.

Meanwhile, toss the cobnuts with the sea salt and oil and spread out on a baking tray. Place in the oven for 3–4 minutes to colour lightly, while the pigeons are cooking.

Transfer the roasted pigeons to a warm plate and set aside to rest. Tip the bacon pieces into the roasting pan and fry over a medium heat for 3–4 minutes until lightly coloured. Remove with a slotted spoon and put to one side. Add a tablespoonful of water to the pan and stir over a low heat for a minute to scrape up any residue from the bottom. Spoon into a small bowl and whisk in the vinegar, mustard, oil and some seasoning to make the dressing.

Take the legs off the pigeon and remove as much meat from them as you can, then shred it. Cut the breasts from the birds with a sharp knife and cut each one into 6 or 7 thin slices.

To serve, toss the leaves with the bacon, dressing and shredded leg meat and divide among serving plates. Arrange the sliced pigeon breasts on top and scatter the cobnuts over. Serve at once.

WOOD PIGEON WITH BLAEBERRIES *serves 4*

Like other game birds, a wood pigeon can easily be overcooked, which is as disastrous as a 'well done' fillet steak. I strongly recommend that whatever you decide to serve with your pigeon, you get it ready almost to the point of serving before you pop the birds into the oven. Don't get caught rushing around putting accompaniments together at the last minute, as the bird will continue to cook as it rests.

4 wood pigeons
salt and freshly ground black pepper
4 sprigs of thyme
100g butter, softened
2 teaspoons plain flour
60ml port
150ml chicken stock
1 small cup of blaeberries (wild blueberries)

Preheat the oven to 220°C/gas 7. Season the pigeons inside and out and put a sprig of thyme inside each cavity with a generous knob of butter. Rub the rest of the butter over the pigeon breasts, then roast the birds for 7–8 minutes. Transfer to a warm platter and set aside.

Add the flour to the roasting pan. Stir in the port, then gradually stir in the stock to avoid lumps forming. Bring to the boil, stirring, and simmer over a medium heat for 4–5 minutes or until the sauce has reduced and thickened. Meanwhile, cut the birds in half and cut away the backbone, leaving just the breasts on the bone with the legs attached (you can take the breasts off the bone if you wish).

Place the pigeon halves in the sauce and add the blaeberries. Cover with a lid and simmer for 3–4 minutes, turning the birds after a minute and keeping them a little pink. Serve with buttered greens or braised cabbage if you prefer.

Tomatoes

With so many varieties of tomatoes on offer these days, it isn't too difficult to come up with a tempting tomato dish. A platter of different fully ripe tomatoes, sliced and drizzled with good oil, finished perhaps with a few nuggets of goat's cheese, is always impressive. And of course there are all manner of soups and sauces that you can create.

If you're a keen tomato grower, you can preserve your excess crop. Halve the tomatoes and semi-dry them in the oven on its lowest setting for a few hours until shrivelled, then preserve in oil in sterilised jars, with a few thyme or other herb sprigs added. These semi-dried tomatoes have all sorts of uses – a great accompaniment to cheese, they can also be chopped and added to salads, sauces and so on. Cherry tomatoes semi-dried with their stalks on make a particularly good snack with drinks.

ICED PLUM TOMATO SOUP WITH HORSERADISH *serves* 4

I suppose this delicious chilled soup is verging on being a bloody Mary – a brunchy hangover soup maybe, or just a clever lunch dish or dinner party starter. I've included some tomato juice here, just to intensify the flavour a little, but if you've got really ripe, great flavoured tomatoes you needn't bother.

250g ripe red tomatoes, halved and deseeded

250g cherry tomatoes

150ml tomato juice

½ garlic clove, peeled and blanched in boiling water for 2 minutes

salt and freshly ground black pepper

FOR THE GARNISH

60–70g mixed tomatoes (red and yellow cherry, plum, etc.)

about 20–30g freshly grated horseradish

2 tablespoons olive oil

Put the ripe tomatoes in a blender with the cherry tomatoes, tomato juice and garlic. Whiz to a purée, then pass through a fine sieve into a bowl. Season with salt and pepper to taste, then chill in the fridge for an hour or two, or the freezer for 20–30 minutes if you're in a hurry.

To serve, divide the soup among chilled soup plates. Cut the mixed tomatoes into even-sized chunks and add to the soup. Scatter the grated horseradish on top and drizzle with the olive oil.

TOMATO AND LOVAGE SALAD *serves 4*

If you have a good selection of tasty tomatoes, you really don't need to do anything too clever to them. Just some torn lovage leaves, and perhaps a few spring onions, is enough to turn them into a simple but special salad.

Like basil, lovage has a way of working itself into dishes to give them a real lift, but it can be overpowering and needs to be used in moderation.

300–400g mixed tomatoes

a few sprigs of lovage

2 tablespoons finely chopped spring onions or chives (optional)

a little malt vinegar or cider vinegar, to drizzle

2–3 tablespoons extra virgin rapeseed oil

sea salt and freshly ground black pepper

Cut the tomatoes into chunks, wedges or halves; leave small ones whole. Arrange on plates and tear the lovage leaves over them. Scatter over the spring onions or chives if using. Drizzle with a little vinegar and oil as desired, and sprinkle with salt and pepper to taste.

FRIED GREEN TOMATOES IN BEER BATTER *serves 4*

The origins of this dish may well lie in South America, where varieties are specifically grown as green tomatoes, but I find it works well with homegrown tomatoes that don't ripen owing to our unreliable weather. Fried in a light batter made with some good old British beer, they make a perfect accompaniment to grilled meats. Alternatively, serve them with a sauce of diced ripe red tomatoes and chopped basil leaves tossed with a little extra virgin rapeseed oil.

4 green tomatoes

vegetable or corn oil for deep-frying

plain flour for dusting

salt

FOR THE BATTER

8 tablespoons self-raising flour

about 200–225ml light beer, such as pale ale, to mix

cayenne pepper

First make the batter. Put the self-raising flour into a bowl and whisk in enough beer to make a smooth, coating batter. Season with salt and cayenne pepper.

Cut the green tomatoes into even slices, about 1cm thick, using a sharp knife.

Heat about an 8cm depth of oil in a deep-fat fryer or other suitable heavy pan to 160–180°C. (Check the temperature with a thermometer.)

You'll need to fry the tomato slices in batches. Dust them with flour, then dip into the batter to coat, lower into the hot oil and fry for 3–4 minutes until golden. Drain on kitchen paper and lightly season with salt.

Serve piping hot.

TOMATOES ON TOAST WITH AGED LANCASHIRE CHEESE *serves* 4

This simple snack is delicious, particularly if you use one of the sweet, tasty heritage varieties or a large juicy beefsteak tomato, though any flavourful tomatoes will do. I'd also recommend a sourdough base and a great cheese, such as the one produced by the Kirkhams in Lancashire.

4 large ripe tomatoes

1 tablespoon rapeseed oil, plus extra to drizzle

1 garlic clove, peeled and roughly crushed

a few sprigs of thyme, leaves only

salt and freshly ground black pepper

4 slices of sourdough bread, 1cm thick

100–120g mature Lancashire cheese

wood sorrel leaves or chives, to garnish

Cut about 6 slices from the centre of each tomato, around ½cm thick, and put to one side.

Chop up the rest of the tomatoes and place in a saucepan with the rapeseed oil, garlic and thyme leaves. Season with salt and pepper and cook, stirring, over a low heat for 2–3 minutes until the tomatoes disintegrate into a pulp.

Toast the sourdough bread on both sides, then spread with the tomato mixture and arrange the slices of tomato on top.

With a swivel vegetable peeler or sharp knife, cut the cheese into shavings and arrange on the tomatoes. Drizzle with a little rapeseed oil and scatter with wood sorrel leaves or chives to serve.

Salmon and sea trout

A freshly caught wild salmon has a magnificent flavour, but there is nothing wrong with a farmed salmon – or sea trout for that matter – provided it has been reared properly. Both salmon and sea trout can be treated in exactly the same way and my preference is always to keep things simple. Often, I'll put a fresh salmon or sea trout into a fish kettle with a few herbs and peppercorns, pour on cold water and slowly bring to the boil, then turn off the heat and leave the fish to cook in the residual heat as it cools. Freshly made hollandaise (see page 74), new potatoes and some steamed spinach are all that's needed for a perfect feast.

Of late, I've become keen on curing and smoking my own fish, especially salmon. It's really quite satisfying and I'm constantly developing new cures. It takes a while to get it right though – some of my earlier cold smokes ended up hot smoked until I got used to my new smoker. Not that anything was wasted – my hot smoked fish got turned into kedgeree, salads and chowder.

FILLET OF SEA TROUT WITH CRUSHED PEAS AND GIROLLES *serves* 4

Peas and fish are a perfect match, and scattering a few girolles or other seasonal wild mushrooms on top makes it even better. I like to crush the peas with a little fish stock so they act rather like a sauce. If you can't find girolles, then any other wild mushroom will do.

4 sea trout fillets (with skin), each about 150g

salt and freshly ground black pepper

1 tablespoon rapeseed oil

a few knobs of butter for frying

150–160g girolles, cleaned

1 tablespoon chopped parsley

FOR THE CRUSHED PEAS

150g podded fresh (or frozen) peas

pinch of sugar

100g butter

1 shallot, peeled and roughly chopped

120–150ml fish stock

First prepare the crushed peas. Cook the peas in boiling salted water with the sugar until almost tender, then drain. Melt half the butter in a pan and gently cook the shallot for a few minutes until softened. Add the peas and stock, season and simmer over a medium heat for 3–4 minutes until most of the stock has evaporated. Tip into a food processor and whiz briefly to a coarse purée, then return to the pan and add the rest of the butter.

Season the fish with salt and pepper. Heat the oil and a knob of butter in a heavy-based frying and cook the fish for 2–3 minutes on each side, depending on thickness.

Meanwhile, heat 2 knobs of butter in another frying pan over a medium heat. Add the girolles and cook for 4–5 minutes until tender, seasoning and adding the parsley halfway through.

To serve, warm the crushed peas if necessary, then spoon onto warm plates. Place the fish fillets on top and spoon the girolles and parsley over and around.

TREACLE CURED SALMON *serves 8–10*

This dish comes from Nigel Howarth of the Three Fishes and Northcote Manor in Lancashire. He served it up at one of his annual food festivals, where he invites chefs from around Britain and further afield to cook for the evening. It can also be made with sea trout.

- 1 salmon fillet (with skin), about 750g–1kg, trimmed
- 80g black treacle
- 1 teaspoon fennel seeds, crushed
- grated zest of 1 lemon
- 50g sea salt
- 1 tablespoon English mustard
- 2 teaspoons coarsely ground black pepper

Lay the salmon fillet skin side down on a sheet of cling film. Warm the treacle in a bowl over a pan of simmering water until it is just runny. Mix the fennel seeds, lemon zest, salt, mustard, pepper and treacle together. Spread evenly over the salmon and wrap well in more cling film. Place on a tray, still skin side down, and leave at room temperature for 1 hour, then refrigerate for 48 hours.

When ready to serve, remove the cling film and scrape away any excess liquid and marinade from the salmon. Pat dry with kitchen paper.

Cut the salmon at a 90° angle to the skin into even slices, about 3mm thick. Serve with pickled cucumber (see right) or pickled samphire, or just some good bread and a leafy salad.

BRADEN ROST SALAD WITH PICKLED CUCUMBER AND HORSERADISH *serves 4*

Braden rost is a traditional way to eat smoked salmon that was most likely invented by mistake. Basically the salmon is cured and smoked traditionally, then finished in a hot kiln. I would imagine that someone had been on the highland brew and accidentally turned up the heat! If you have a home smoker then you could create it yourself using a cure of sea salt and unrefined brown sugar, or simply buy it ready done.

½ cucumber

1–2 teaspoons rapeseed oil

salt and freshly ground black pepper

8 spring onions, trimmed

300–400g piece Braden rost (hot smoked salmon)

2–3 handfuls of small salad leaves, such as baby spinach, pea shoots, ruby chard, rocket and red mustard leaf, washed and dried

100–120g pickled cucumber (see right)

a few chives, snipped

FOR THE CIDER DRESSING

1 tablespoon cider vinegar

1 teaspoon clear honey

1 teaspoon grain mustard

2 tablespoons rapeseed oil

2 tablespoons vegetable or corn oil

For the cider dressing, whisk all of the ingredients together in a bowl and season with salt and pepper to taste. Set aside.

Cut the fresh cucumber on the diagonal into ½cm thick slices. Heat the rapeseed oil in a frying pan and sauté the cucumber slices for 3–4 minutes, seasoning and turning them every so often, until lightly coloured. Remove with a slotted spoon and set aside.

Cut the spring onions into 3–4cm lengths and sauté in the same pan for 2–3 minutes until lightly coloured. Take off the heat.

Remove the skin from the salmon and break the flesh into pieces. Toss the salad leaves in the dressing, season lightly and divide among serving plates. Arrange the salmon, pickled and sautéed cucumbers, spring onions and chives in among the leaves and drizzle over any remaining dressing.

PICKLED CUCUMBER *serves 4–6*

1 medium cucumber

1 tablespoon good quality white wine vinegar

grated zest of 1 lemon

2 tablespoons rapeseed oil

good pinch of salt

2 tablespoons chopped dill

Halve the cucumber lengthways and scoop out the seeds, then cut the flesh into 3mm slices and place in a bowl. Add the wine vinegar, lemon zest, rapeseed oil, salt and dill and toss to mix. Cover and leave to stand for about 45 minutes before serving.

HONEY ROAST SEA TROUT WITH FENNEL *serves 4–6*

This is a great way to cook sea trout or salmon for a party. It's very easy and has quite an unusual but delicious taste. You can use a fillet of any size – just up the cooking time slightly for a larger fish. And if you happen to have an outside brick oven, it will be perfect for cooking this dish. Serve as a starter or main dish, or as part of a selection of dishes for a party.

1 sea trout fillet (with skin), about 500g

a little rapeseed oil

salt and freshly ground black pepper

2–3 tablespoons clear honey

1 tablespoon grainy mustard

2–3 tablespoons chopped fennel tops or dill

Preheat the oven to 230°C/gas 8. Place the fish on a lightly oiled baking tray and season with salt and pepper. Mix the honey, mustard and fennel together (you can do this in a small food processor if you wish) and spread evenly over the fish.

Bake for about 10–15 minutes, basting the fish every so often until just cooked. Serve hot or warm.

Blueberries

Native blueberries are not as sought after as, say, strawberries and raspberries, and we tend to rely on imports rather than cultivate our own. Their uses in the kitchen are, however, just as interesting, though they rarely get exploited to the full. If anything, blueberries – especially wild ones – probably have more possibilities in savoury dishes than their rivals. Added at the last minute, they give a lovely sweet and sour taste to sauces to enhance duck and game dishes.

Obviously, you can add blueberries to all kinds of sweet dishes, including fruit salads and compotes. One of my favourite ways to eat them is piled onto drop scones or pancakes and drizzled with some good honey for breakfast. And in health terms, the blueberry is right up there as a super food, so a glass of freshly blended blueberry juice is a powerful way to start your day.

BURNT CREAM WITH BLUEBERRIES *serves* 4

Whether this simple dessert is of British, French or Spanish origin is a matter of debate. One thing for sure, it's best made with the most luxurious cream you can buy.

600ml thick Jersey cream

8 egg yolks

75g unrefined caster sugar

120g blueberries

The day before serving, bring the cream to the boil in a heavy-based pan. Meanwhile, in a bowl, mix the egg yolks with 1 tablespoon caster sugar. Pour the cream on to the egg yolks, whisking well. Return to the pan and cook over a low heat, stirring constantly with a wooden spoon, until the mixture thickens enough to coat the back of the spoon; don't let it boil. Set aside to cool a little.

Scatter the blueberries evenly in a large gratin dish or 4 ramekins or other shallow individual heatproof dishes. Pour the cream mixture over them and refrigerate overnight until set.

An hour before serving, sprinkle the rest of the sugar over the cream to form an even layer. Spray with a little water and caramelise with a cook's blowtorch (or under the grill preheated to its maximum setting). Set aside at cool room temperature, or chill until ready to serve.

BLUEBERRY MERINGUES *serves* 4

Cream, meringue and berries are perfect partners. I've used blueberries here, although any singular berry or a mixture would be just fine. When you're preparing meringue, make sure that all of your equipment is very clean and dry. Any trace of grease or oil will prevent the meringue from whipping to a really stiff consistency.

3 egg whites

100g caster sugar

1 teaspoon cornflour

1 teaspoon white wine vinegar

TO SERVE

2 tablespoons caster sugar

½ tablespoon water

300–350g blueberries

200ml double cream

a few drops of vanilla extract

Preheat the oven to 100°C/gas ¼ or as low as it will go. Using an electric whisk, beat the egg whites in a large bowl until stiff. Whisk in the caster sugar a spoonful at a time and continue whisking until the meringue is really stiff and shiny. Add the cornflour and vinegar and whisk again for about 30 seconds or until stiff and shiny again.

Line a large baking tray with baking parchment, then spoon the meringue into 8 thin rounds, about 7–8cm in diameter and no more than 1cm thick.

Cook in the oven for an hour or so until the meringue rounds are crisp on the outside and a little soft in the middle, but don't let them colour – you want them nice and white. They make take a little longer, depending on your oven. Remove and set aside to cool.

Meanwhile, dissolve 1 tablespoon of the caster sugar in the water in a saucepan. Put 50g of the blueberries into a blender, add the sugar syrup and blend to a purée. Whip the cream with the vanilla extract and remaining 1 tablespoon sugar.

To assemble, place each meringue disc on a serving plate and spoon on a layer of cream. Scatter with the remaining blueberries and spoon on the blueberry purée. Place another meringue disc on top and serve.

BLUEBERRY CHEESECAKE *serves* 4

A truly comforting dessert. I've used blueberries here, but you could substitute raspberries, blackcurrants or strawberries, adjusting the sweetness accordingly.

450g blueberries, hulled

200g caster sugar

200ml water

20g cornflour

FOR THE BASE

250g digestive biscuits or Hobnobs

80g butter, melted

FOR THE FILLING

300ml double cream

100g caster sugar

500g cream cheese, such as Philadelphia

finely grated zest of 1 lemon

1 teaspoon vanilla extract

Put 200g of the (softer) blueberries into a pan with the sugar and 175ml water. Heat slowly to dissolve the sugar, then simmer for 7–8 minutes. Mix the cornflour with the remaining 25ml water and stir into the mixture. Simmer, stirring, for 2–3 minutes. Strain through a fine sieve into a bowl, pressing the berries in the sieve to extract as much juice as possible. Leave to cool.

Line a 17–18cm springform cake tin with greaseproof paper. Crush the biscuits in a food processor to coarse crumbs. (Or put in a plastic bag and smash with a rolling pin.) Mix with the melted butter and pack into the cake tin to make the base, firming with the back of a spoon.

Whip the cream and sugar together until fairly stiff. In another bowl, beat the cream cheese to soften, then fold in the cream with the lemon zest and vanilla extract. Lightly fold through half of the blueberry syrup to create a rippled effect. Spoon the mix onto the biscuit base and place in the fridge for 2–3 hours until firm.

Mix the rest of the fruit with the remaining blueberry syrup. To unmould the cheesecake, run a hot knife around the edge, then release the side of the tin and slide the cheesecake onto a board. Cut into slices and serve each one topped with a generous spoonful of blueberry sauce.

September

Sweet, succulent PRAWNS, *wild mushrooms of every description, colourful* SQUASHES and PUMPKINS *and dark, juicy* AUTUMN BERRIES *plucked from hedgerows...*

 OTHER INGREDIENTS NOT TO BE MISSED

Wild salmon   Sea trout   Red mullet   Crayfish   Sprats   Mussels   Cockles   Native oysters

Mallard   Grouse   Snipe   Teal   Widgeon   Ptarmigan   Beetroot   Chard   Celery   Swede   Water celery

Bittercress   Pennywort   Nasturtiums   Tomatoes   Elderberries   Crab apples   Wild cherry plums   Pears

Hazelnuts   Walnuts   Cobnuts

September is an interesting month, when summer can either turn cool and stormy, or stay the course. Consequently, summer produce can either continue or come to a fairly abrupt end. Weather apart, it's an exciting time of the year, because you can feast on autumnal game and still manage to harvest summer berries. I keep menus simple now, usually offering wild mushrooms as a starter, followed by a game bird, with an autumn fruit dessert to finish. I know that I tend to talk foraging and hunting a lot, but this is the month when I really look forward to being invited to Scotland to fish, forage and shoot. You can catch your salmon, shoot your grouse and forage for your third course or garnish.

Foraging for mushrooms can be as dependent on the elements as fishing. It all depends on the weather, moon and probably some kind of earth gravity thing! I have been picking wild mushrooms for years and just love coming across the different varieties as they appear – or not as is sometimes the case. I'll often re-visit a spot where I've stumbled across a bumper crop the previous year and find nothing. That's the magic of the mushroom. No one really understands why they appear erratically in some places and never return. At least if all fails, you still get some exercise and fresh air.

As a kid, I used to get plenty of fresh sea air at this time of the year – prawning on the end of West Bay pier. A local fisherman and net maker kindly made me proper prawn nets to replace the recycled bicycle wheel I had been using, and for bait I used to scrounge fish that was on its last legs from the local fish merchant, Samways. Straight after school I'd be out on the pier along with my mates, tilley lamps and flasks of tea in hand. Often we'd just catch enough for

a sandwich, but occasionally we would net a few pounds and try to sell them to the local pub landlord. Back then, prawns were just cooked and peeled for a sandwich or eaten in their natural state. Now, they get served in a silver tankard and dipped into proper top notch homemade mayonnaise, or deep-fried in their shells.

This is also the time of the year when winter squashes start appearing alongside good old marrows – the last of the summer squashes. Pumpkins and squashes are fascinating, though most of them are more appealing to the eye than to peel, prep and eat. In my opinion, you can't go wrong with butternut squash. Don't be put off by its odd shape and thick skin, which admittedly is a little tough to remove, as butternut flesh has the most delicious flavour and texture. With the other varieties, you won't really know how good they are until you get them home and start chopping. Their eating quality is hidden beneath the skin and mainly down to ripeness – rather like their relative the melon. That said, it is well worth sampling some of the hundred or so squashes available – ask your greengrocer or farmers' market stallholders to recommend varieties when they are at their best.

The brightly coloured fruits of the summer months now make way for the deeper, darker berries of the autumn – blackberries, loganberries, tayberries and blueberries, which are still around. Their mauve and blue hues really give desserts a sense of the season. Unlike red fruits, which can more or less be served as they are, autumn berries generally benefit from a little cooking, so they make that turn in seasonal cookery a little easier.

Prawns

The prawns caught around our coastline, especially in the Southwest, have a unique sweet flavour, but we are so used to buying imported prawns that we tend to forget the natives, or at least our fishmongers do. They become available as our water gets colder, from late August through September and October. Ok, they are smaller and not as plentiful as the imports, but if you do manage to get your hands on some, they are a bit of a treat. I often serve them freshly cooked and still warm in a half pint mug, with some good mayonnaise or cocktail sauce, or deep-fried in their shells (see page 153). If, on the other hand, your preference is the ubiquitous prawn cocktail, then using freshly cooked and peeled prawns will make the world of difference.

TO COOK LIVE PRAWNS: simply drop them into a large pan of fast-boiling well-salted water and cook until they turn pink, about 2–3 minutes after the water returns to the boil. Drain, cool, then peel off the shells, but don't throw them in the bin. Instead, use the shells to make a tasty stock (as in the recipe below), to flavour a soup or sauce to accompany a fish main course.

PAN-FRIED DABS WITH PRAWNS *serves* 4

Dabs are one of those fish that you rarely find at fishmongers. I imagine that most of them get dumped or used for pot bait… and there lies the problem with fishing. As consumers, we don't get to see the fish that go back, yet small flat fish like dabs, sand soles, megrim, etc., make good eating and their flesh is easily removed from the bone. Adding some peeled prawns turns a humble fish like dab into a luxury dish.

200–250g prawns, cooked and peeled, shells reserved

8 dabs, trimmed of their fins and dark skin removed

salt and freshly ground black pepper

plain flour for dusting

2–3 tablespoons vegetable or rapeseed oil

150g unsalted butter

2 tablespoons chopped parsley

juice of ½ lemon

Place the prawn shells in a saucepan and add enough water to just cover them. Bring to the boil, lower the heat and simmer for about 10 minutes until the liquid has reduced right down, then strain through a fine sieve into a bowl; set aside.

Season the dabs and lightly flour them. Heat the oil in two large frying pans (or use one pan and cook in two batches). Add the dabs to the pan(s) and fry over a medium heat for about 2–3 minutes on each side until they begin to colour. Add half the butter and continue to cook for another couple of minutes. Remove the fish from the pan and keep warm.

Add the prawn stock to the pan with the peeled prawns, then add the rest of the butter and chopped parsley. Season lightly and keep on a low heat for a minute, then add the lemon juice.

Arrange the dabs on warm plates and spoon the prawns and butter over them. Serve at once.

FRIED PRAWNS AND SAND EELS *serves* 4

Our small native prawns are ideal for deep-frying whole in a light batter, as the shells become perfectly edible. You may think that sounds nuts, but I've experienced much purer prawn eating in Tokyo where they serve you live peeled prawns straight from the tank and then bring you back the shells that have been deep-fried and scattered with sea salt!

I've mixed them here with sand eels, which I often use when I'm fishing as live bait to catch sea bass, though they are delicious deep-fried. I suggest you serve this English seaside version of *fritto misto* with a tartare sauce – good homemade mayonnaise flavoured with chopped capers, gherkins and chopped parsley.

160g small raw or cooked prawns
(in the shell)

120g self-raising flour

sea salt

a good pinch of cayenne pepper

200ml milk

vegetable or corn oil for deep-frying

150g sand eels

1 lemon, cut into 4 wedges

Rinse the prawns and pat thoroughly dry. Season the flour with salt and cayenne pepper. Have three bowls or shallow dishes ready, one containing the flour, one with the milk and a third to take the coated prawns and eels. Heat an 8cm depth of oil in a deep-fat fryer or other suitable heavy-based saucepan to 160–180°C.

A handful at a time, dip the prawns into the flour, shaking off any excess back into the bowl. Then pass them through the milk, draining off any excess, and then again through the flour. Put the prawns into the third dish. Do exactly the same with the sand eels, then mix with the prawns.

Deep-fry the prawns and sand eels, a handful or so at a time, for 3–4 minutes or until golden. Remove with a slotted spoon and drain on kitchen paper. Lightly season with a little more salt and serve at once, with lemon wedges for squeezing.

PRAWN COCKTAIL *serves* 4

This Seventies must-have menu item is still incredibly popular. There's something about the sauce that makes even the worst frozen prawns taste acceptable. But if you take it up a few notches by using fresh prawns, perhaps adding some langoustines and/or fresh crab meat, spicing up the sauce a little, and adding some finely diced cucumber, you can create a truly luxury seafood cocktail. Here's the basic recipe – add in extra seafood as you like.

½ small cucumber

1 small head of romaine or Cos lettuce,
trimmed and washed

1 head of Belgium endive (or chicory),
trimmed

4 spring onions, trimmed and finely
shredded

400–500g prawns, cooked and peeled

4 whole cooked prawns (in shell), to
garnish

1 lemon or lime, quartered, to serve

FOR THE SAUCE

5 tablespoons good quality mayonnaise
(preferably homemade, see page 119)

5 tablespoons tomato ketchup

2 teaspoons Worcestershire sauce

a few drops of Tabasco

1 tablespoon creamed horseradish or
freshly grated horseradish

½ tablespoon Pernod or Ricard

½ tablespoon chopped dill

salt and freshly ground black pepper

Peel the skin from the cucumber, then cut in half lengthways and scoop out the seeds. Finely dice the flesh and place in a large bowl. Shred the lettuce and endive finely and add to the cucumber with the spring onions.

To make the sauce, mix the mayonnaise together with all the rest of the ingredients, seasoning with salt and pepper to taste.

To serve, put a spoonful of the sauce into each cocktail glass or individual glass serving bowls. Divide the salad among the glasses, then arrange the prawns on top and coat with the sauce. Garnish each serving with a whole prawn and serve with lemon or lime wedges.

Wild mushrooms

These are increasingly popular in this country and, when they are in season, you can often find a selection in specialist greengrocers and even supermarkets. Better still, you can forage for them – it's a fun weekend activity and a great excuse to get into the woods for a country walk. A word of warning though, most forests demand a licence these days and limit the weight you pick, so check it out first.

There are about five or six mushroom varieties that I concentrate on during the year, which can be foraged fairly easily depending on conditions. Oyster, cep, chanterelle, trompette, hedgehog fungus and puffball mushrooms are all quite common in the UK and they are very versatile. At dinner parties where a couple of friends are vegetarian, I'll sometimes just serve a plate of ceps roasted with garlic as a main dish – no one seems to notice that there isn't any meat on the menu. Mushrooms really do go well with almost anything savoury.

The first thing I do when I return from an early morning foraging mission is to fry some and eat them on toast or in an omelette. Depending on the harvest, our mushroom bounty will sometimes keep us going for a week.

PUFFBALL WITH WILD MUSHROOMS
serves 4

Puffball mushrooms are a strange phenomenon. They appear at the most unexpected times – any time from July to October depending on the weather. Puffballs are inspirational to cook with. You can dice them and use them in a mixture of mushrooms, or slice them and use them as a base in place of toast – for whatever you like really – this is my favourite way to eat them. They are especially good as a breakfast dish.

If you're lucky enough to find a puffball, make sure it is pure white with no yellow patches and very firm. If it's very large you may need to halve it before slicing.

3–4 tablespoons rapeseed oil

4 slices of puffball, cut about 2cm thick

salt and freshly ground black pepper

120g butter

2 large shallots, peeled, halved and finely chopped

2 garlic cloves, peeled and crushed

400–500g seasonal wild mushrooms, cleaned and cut into even-sized pieces

2 tablespoons chopped parsley

Heat 2 tablespoons of the rapeseed oil in a large frying pan and cook the puffball slices for 3–4 minutes on each side until nicely coloured, seasoning them during cooking and adding a little more oil if the pan becomes dry. Add a knob of butter towards the end of cooking. Tip into a warm dish, cover and keep warm.

Heat another tablespoon of rapeseed oil in the same pan with a good knob of butter and gently cook the shallots and garlic for a couple of minutes without colouring. Add the wild mushrooms, season and cook over a medium heat for 4–5 minutes until they soften, then add the rest of the butter and the chopped parsley.

To serve, place a puffball slice on each warm plate and spoon the mushrooms on top.

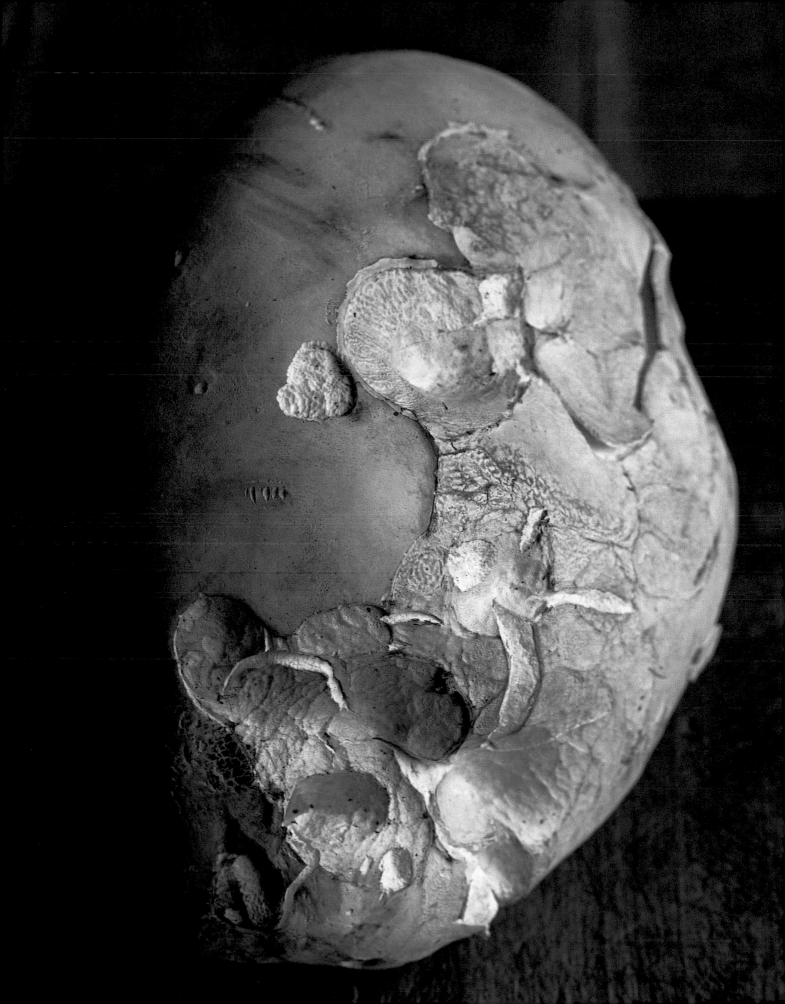

RAY WITH PERIWINKLES AND CEPS

serves 4

Rays, commonly referred to as skate in fishmongers, are among my favourite eating fish. Here I've teamed them with winkles and ceps to give a complete earthy dish. You may need to order a sustainable ray (spotted, cuckoo or starry) and fresh winkles from your fishmonger in advance. And, if you can't find or forage ceps, then replace them with another wild mushroom.

    4 ray (or skate) wings, each about
    200–250g, skinned

    150–200g fresh winkles

    salt and freshly ground white pepper

    plain flour for dusting

    vegetable or corn oil for frying

    150g unsalted butter

    150–160g ceps, cleaned and sliced

    1 tablespoon chopped parsley

Trim the ray (or skate) wings and set aside. Wash the winkles, place them in a saucepan and cover with salted water. Bring to the boil and simmer for 5–6 minutes, then drain and leave to cool. Using a cocktail stick, prise out the meat from the winkle shells and remove the little hard 'foot' attached to the meat, which is too tough to eat.

Season the ray wings and lightly flour them. Heat a thin film of oil in a heavy-based or non-stick frying pan and cook the wings for 3–5 minutes on each side until golden. Just before they are cooked, add about a third of the butter to the pan and continue to fry for about a minute to give them a nice brown colour. When they are done, remove them from the pan and keep warm. If your pan isn't large enough to cook them all at once, brown them two at a time. The first two can be finished off in a hot oven, preheated to 200°C/gas 6, for about 10 minutes – the time it will take to cook the other two in the pan.

Wipe the pan out with some kitchen paper (or use a clean pan). Add half the remaining butter and cook the ceps over a medium heat for a few minutes, turning them until lightly coloured. Add the rest of the butter, the winkles and chopped parsley and heat for 1–2 minutes.

Place a ray wing on each warm plate and spoon the contents of the pan evenly over the top. Serve with spinach and good buttery mash.

ROAST PARTRIDGE WITH WILD MUSHROOMS AND AUTUMN GREENS

serves 4

Partridge is a mild-flavoured game bird, which often suits those who would normally steer clear of game. Earthy ceps and tender autumn leaves complete the dish.

    4 oven-ready partridges

    salt and freshly ground black pepper

    about 100g butter

    1 small head of greens, such as sprout
    tops or Savoy cabbage, woody stalks
    removed and cut into even-sized pieces

    200–250g wild mushrooms, cleaned and
    cut into even-sized pieces, or left whole
    if chanterelles

Preheat the oven to 220°C/gas 7. Season the partridges inside and out with salt and pepper and rub with butter. Place the birds in a roasting tray, in which they fit snugly, and cook for 15 minutes, basting every so often.

Around halfway through cooking, bring a pan of lightly salted water to the boil and cook the greens for about 6–7 minutes until tender, then drain.

Meanwhile, heat a little more butter in a frying pan and cook the mushrooms over a medium heat for a few minutes, seasoning halfway through cooking.

To serve, toss the greens and mushrooms together, adjust the seasoning and add a knob of butter if you like. Serve the partridge whole, cut in half or off the bone, with the greens and mushrooms.

Squashes, pumpkins and marrows

This motley family, with its wonderful variety of shapes and colours, is probably the most interesting and unusual of all vegetables. Beyond Halloween lanterns, pumpkins and squashes deserve to be used much more as a vegetable – in the way the Italians do.

Butternut squash is the variety I usually choose to prepare and cook, as it has a good flavour and texture. I find a serrated bread knife is often the best tool for cutting away its hard skin.

Most squashes and pumpkins can be used in much the same way as root vegetables – in soups, mashed or baked. Try roasting chunks and wedges of different squashes in the oven drizzled with olive oil, then just finish with grated orange or lemon zest and a good grinding of salt and pepper. Baked squashes are also great with some cobnuts thrown in at the end. Or, once baked, you can grate some mature cheese like Cheddar or Lancashire over them and flash them under the grill.

You can even use these vegetables for desserts – American-style pumpkin pie can be delicious and I've even made a chocolate and pumpkin pie.

ROAST AUTUMN SQUASH AND WALNUT SOUP *serves 4*

Closer-textured orange-fleshed squash – like butternut and onion – are particularly good for soups. These varieties tend to have a better ratio of usable flesh to skin than some of the larger squashes and pumpkins. Fresh walnuts are around this month and make a natural crunchy accompaniment.

1kg butternut or onion squash

a large knob of butter

1 small leek, trimmed, chopped and washed

1 small onion, peeled and roughly chopped

about 1.2 litres vegetable stock

salt and freshly ground black pepper

1 tablespoon pumpkin seeds, lightly toasted

12–15 fresh walnuts, shelled and roughly broken

Peel the squash, halve and remove the seeds and fibrous bits, then roughly chop the flesh. Heat the butter in a large saucepan and gently cook the leek and onion for 4–5 minutes until softened.

Add the squash and stock, bring to the boil and season with salt and pepper. Leave to simmer for 20 minutes. Scoop out a spoonful of the cubed squash, using a slotted spoon, and reserve for serving.

Whiz the soup in a blender if necessary until smooth, then strain through a fine sieve back into the pan. Reheat gently, stirring in a little more vegetable stock or water if the soup is too thick. Taste and adjust the seasoning.

Pour the soup into warm soup plates and add the reserved squash cubes. Top with a light sprinkling of toasted pumpkin seeds and walnut pieces and serve straight away.

SLOW-COOKED PORK BELLY
WITH AUTUMN SQUASH *serves* 4

Pork belly is one of the tastiest cuts to slow roast, especially if you can get your hands on a rare breed like Saddleback, Old Spot or Middle White. Their bellies may look a little more fatty, but the fat renders down during cooking, to give you a very fine piece of roast meat.

Ask your butcher to remove the bones, which can be cooked as spare ribs or simply used as a trivet to cook the pork on.

1 piece of boneless pork belly with rind, about 1–1.5kg

salt and freshly ground black pepper

a few sprigs of rosemary, chopped

1 tablespoon crushed fennel seeds

rapeseed oil for basting

1kg mixed squashes, such as acorn, onion and butternut

Preheat the oven to 230°C/gas 8. Using a Stanley knife or a razor-sharp knife, score lines about ½cm apart across the pork belly rind.

Put the pork belly in a large roasting tray and pour in about a 2cm depth of water. Place on the hob and bring to the boil, then lower the heat and simmer for a couple of minutes. Remove from the heat and pour off the water.

Season the pork belly with salt and pepper, then rub the rosemary and fennel seeds into the scored rind and over the flesh. Spoon over a little rapeseed oil and roast for 30 minutes. Turn the oven down to 160°C/gas 3 and cook for a further 2–2½ hours, basting the meat every so often and draining off excess fat from the tin.

Meanwhile, prepare the squashes. Peel those with thicker skins. Cut all of them into even-sized chunks and wedges, discarding the seeds and fibrous bits. Season the squash and tip into the roasting tray around the pork. Spoon over some of the pork fat in the tray and roast for about another hour, basting every so often.

To serve, cut the pork into 1cm thick slices and arrange on warm plates or a large serving dish with the roasted squash. Accompany with crab apple sauce (see below) or a normal apple sauce.

CRAB APPLE SAUCE

Where I live, the roads are lined with old fruit trees, many of which are crab apple. I've discovered that the trees with much larger oval-shaped fruit are either Dartmouth or John Downie varieties. More user-friendly in the kitchen, these crab apples make an excellent sauce – an ideal alternative to the normal apple sauce.

To make crab apple sauce, wash and de-stalk about 500g crab apples, (preferably one of the larger varieties). Place in a heavy-based pan with about 100g sugar and a little water. Heat slowly, then simmer with the lid on for about 20 minutes, stirring every so often. Remove the lid and continue cooking until the apples disintegrate and reduce to a sauce-like consistency. Taste for sweetness, adding more sugar if necessary.

MARROW WITH BACON AND HERBS
serves 4–6

Marrow doesn't really get used that much, except for the occasional attempts to stuff it when, more often than not, all you can really taste is the stuffing. However, if it is treated in the right way, it can have good results. This is a tasty dish to serve as an accompaniment to meat and fish dishes.

1 young marrow, about 1kg

salt and freshly ground black pepper

2–3 tablespoons rapeseed oil

a couple of good knobs of butter

1 medium onion, peeled, halved and finely chopped

4 garlic cloves, peeled and crushed

4 rashers of streaky bacon, finely chopped

1 teaspoon thyme leaves

60g fresh white breadcrumbs

3 tablespoons chopped parsley

a few sprigs of tarragon, finely chopped

Halve the marrow lengthways, then scoop out the seeds with a spoon and discard. Cut the marrow into ½cm thick slices. Lay these on a tray, scatter lightly with salt and leave for an hour. Drain the marrow in a colander and pat dry with kitchen paper.

Heat the rapeseed oil in a large frying pan. Season the marrow with pepper, add to the pan and cook over a high heat for 3–4 minutes, turning every so often until lightly coloured and tender.

Meanwhile, heat the butter in a heavy-based saucepan. Add the onion, garlic, bacon and thyme, and cook gently for 3–4 minutes until the onion is soft and the bacon is cooked. Stir in the breadcrumbs, parsley and tarragon, and season with salt and pepper to taste.

Preheat the grill to medium. Transfer the marrow to a serving dish (suitable for use under the grill). Scatter the breadcrumb mixture over the top and place under the grill until lightly browned. Serve immediately.

Autumn fruits

Along with other autumnal fruits, like plums, apples and pears, dark autumn berries, such as blackberries, tayberries and loganberries, will happily slip into most dessert concoctions – from hearty steamed puddings and crumbles to light, healthy fruit salads and compote.

Being a jelly freak, I often continue the berry jelly theme into autumn, using a different flavouring as a base – like wine, cider, Perry or maybe even a touch of last year's sloe gin.

With hedgerow fruits like blackberries you can often end up with a glut after a good foraging session. Fortunately, they freeze well – either whole or puréed. Later in the year, defrost and use in crumbles, or whiz into an autumn fruit smoothie or milk shake. Also, freeze some small tubs of purée – to pop straight into a glass of bubbly for an autumn Champagne cocktail.

SWEET PICKLED GREENGAGES
makes enough to fill four or five 500ml kilner jars

Don't miss out on these lovely little green plums with their sweet-scented flesh at this time of the year. My friend Charles Campion brought me a couple jars of these pickled greengages as a gift a couple of years ago. Having wild fruits on your doorstep is one of the great things about living in the country.

For this recipe, you need to select slightly under-ripe gages, as ripe ones will just disintegrate during storage.

2kg firm greengages, washed
seeds from 20 cardamom pods
5g mace blades
12 dried red chillies
2 tablespoons green peppercorns
1 litre distilled white vinegar
500g granulated or caster sugar

Halve and stone the greengages and pack them into sterilised kilner or preserving jars (500ml capacity). Distribute the spices equally between the jars. You may need more or less fruit, depending how tightly the jars are packed.

Put the vinegar and sugar into a pan and heat gently to dissolve the sugar, stirring a few times. Bring to the boil and boil for a couple of minutes.

Pour the hot vinegar syrup over the fruit in the jars, cover with vinegar-proof lids, then turn the jars upside down for 15 minutes or so (to seal the lids). Turn the jars the right way up again and leave to cool.

Store in a cool, dark place for up to 6 months. I've kept mine for longer in the fridge, so I suggest you put one or two jars in the fridge and open these last.

AUTUMN BERRY PUDDING *serves* 4

It doesn't need to be deep midwinter to appreciate a steamed fruit pudding. When there is an abundance of our autumnal soft fruits around, I like making puddings like this, using dark autumnal fruits that are plentiful in the hedgerows – like blackberries, blueberries, tayberries, loganberries, and perhaps even a few elderberries.

125g butter, softened, plus extra for greasing

125g caster sugar

2 medium eggs (at room temperature), beaten

125g self-raising flour, sifted

80ml milk

300g mixed autumn berries, such as blackberries, blueberries, elderberries, tayberries

60g sugar

150ml port

Preheat the oven to 190°C/gas 5. Butter 4 individual heatproof pudding bowls or pots.

Beat the butter and caster sugar together in a bowl until light and fluffy, then gradually beat in the eggs a little at a time. Carefully fold the flour into the mixture, alternately with the milk, until smooth.

Divide about a third of the berries evenly between the prepared moulds, then spoon the mixture over them to three-quarters fill the moulds. Cover each one with a piece of foil, pleated in the middle, to allow room for expansion. Secure tightly under the rim with string.

Stand the pudding moulds in a deepish baking tray or ovenproof dish and surround with enough boiling water to come about halfway up the sides of the moulds. Cook in the oven for 35–40 minutes until the puddings are springy to the touch.

Meanwhile, dissolve the sugar in the port in a pan over a medium-low heat, then bring to the boil. Add the rest of the berries and heat until just warmed through, stirring them carefully.

To serve, run a knife around the puddings, then turn out onto warm serving plates and spoon the berries and sauce over them. Serve with thick Jersey cream or custard.

AUTUMN FRUIT AND NUT CRUMBLE
serves 4

There are lots of fruits and nuts around now that lend themselves to a tasty crumble. I've added plums to a mix of pears and apples here, but you could use all apples or pears and add a couple of handfuls of autumn berries.

500g cooking apples

500g firm, ripe pears

6–8 plums, quartered and stoned

3 tablespoons caster sugar

FOR THE TOPPING

160g plain flour

80g cold butter, cut into small pieces

90g soft brown sugar

50g oats

60–80g shelled nuts, such as walnuts, hazelnuts, cobnuts or almonds, coarsely chopped

3 tablespoons pumpkin seeds

Preheat the oven to 190°C/gas 5. Peel, halve and core the apples and pears, then cut into large chunks and place in an ovenproof dish. Add the plums and sugar and toss to mix. Cover the dish with a lid or foil and cook in the oven for 30 minutes.

Meanwhile, prepare the crumble topping. Put the flour into a bowl, add the pieces of butter and rub in with your fingertips to give a breadcrumb-like consistency. Add the brown sugar, oats, chopped nuts and pumpkin seeds, and mix well.

Take the dish from the oven and scatter the crumble topping evenly over the fruit. Bake, uncovered, for 30–40 minutes until the topping is nicely coloured.

Serve the crumble with thick cream or custard.

PEAR AND APPLE COBBLER WITH BERRIES serves 4–6

This is pure comfort food – especially if you serve it with thick cream or custard. Vary the fruit according to what you have to hand but do try to include a few handfuls of berries to give some colour.

1 medium cooking apple

2 pears

120g caster sugar

200g plums

200g blueberries

200g blackberries

FOR THE COBBLER

85g unsalted butter, softened

110g caster sugar

220g strong plain flour, plus extra for dusting

½ teaspoon baking powder

a good pinch of salt

100ml milk

1 small egg, beaten

Peel, core and roughly chop the apple and pears and place in a heavy-based saucepan with the sugar. Cook over a low heat for 5–6 minutes with the lid on, stirring every so often, until the apple begins to break down. Add the plums and continue to cook for another 5–6 minutes. Remove from the heat and leave to cool for about 10 minutes. Preheat the oven to 190°C/gas 5.

Meanwhile, make the cobbler dough. In a food mixer or by hand, cream the butter and sugar together until very pale and fluffy. Sift the flour, baking powder and salt over the mixture and fold in, with a little of the milk, until well combined. Gradually incorporate the rest of the milk to give a sticky dough.

Flour your hands and form the cobbler dough into 16–20 small rough balls. Place them on a non-stick baking sheet, brush with the beaten egg and bake in the oven for 6–7 minutes.

Stir the blueberries and blackberries into the fruit mixture and transfer to a large ovenproof serving dish. Arrange the part-baked cobbler balls on top of the fruit mixture and bake for 35–40 minutes until they are golden in colour.

Serve hot, with thick cream or custard.

AUTUMN FRUITS WITH SLOE GIN AND CREAMY RICE PUDDING serves 4

If you're a fan of sloe gin, then you might like to experiment with it in recipes. Here it is used rather like mulled wine, and you can add as little or as much as you wish. If you haven't any sloe gin, then substitute a fruity full-bodied red wine, using 300ml in place of the water and gin.

The choice of fruit is up to you – any plums will work, even greengages, and you can add pears, peeled and cut into wedges if you like. There are often late berries like loganberries still on the bush, the more the merrier.

FOR THE RICE PUDDING

50g pudding rice

25g caster sugar

pinch of freshly grated nutmeg

300ml milk

75ml evaporated milk

75ml thick Jersey or double cream

FOR THE FRUITS

200ml water

½ vanilla pod, split

4 cloves

1 bay leaf

120g brown sugar

a few strips of orange peel

100ml sloe gin, or to taste

200–250g blackberries, elderberries or blueberries

4 ripe plums, quartered and stoned

For the pudding, put the rice, sugar, nutmeg and milk in a pan and bring to the boil. Lower the heat and simmer for 20 minutes until the rice is tender, stirring from time to time. Add the evaporated milk, bring back to the boil and simmer gently for another 10 minutes. Transfer to a bowl and leave to cool.

Once the rice is cold, stir in the cream. Cover and leave in the fridge to set.

For the fruits, pour the water into a pan, add the vanilla, cloves, bay leaf, brown sugar and orange peel, and bring to the boil. Lower the heat and simmer gently for 7–8 minutes, then tip into a bowl and set aside to infuse and cool.

When the syrup is cold, add the sloe gin to taste, then pour over the fruits. Cover and leave for at least 2 hours, stirring occasionally.

Serve the macerated fruits at room temperature, with the rice pudding.

October

Old forgotten BEETROOT
varieties, freshly dug ONIONS
in all shapes and sizes, and
beautiful heritage APPLES
enjoying a welcome revival...

OTHER INGREDIENTS NOT TO BE MISSED

Pheasant   Partridge   Grouse   Wild ducks   Wild rabbit   Hare   Parsnips   Swede   Turnips   Celeriac

Carrots   Red cabbage   Autumn greens   Shallots   Jerusalem artichokes   Celery   Chicory

Marrows   Spinach   Leeks   Squashes   Pumpkins   Horseradish root   Chickweed   Lovage   Pennywort

Wild sorrel   Wood sorrel   Wild chervil   Dittander   Laver   Chanterelles   Ceps   Beefsteak fungus

Horn of plenty   Puffball   Hedgehog fungus   Charcoal burners   Nasturtiums   Blackberries   Sloes

Pears   Crab apples   Elderberries   Blackberries   Hazelnuts   Chestnuts   Cobnuts   Walnuts

October is the month when all I seem to do is sweep up and bag leaves to compost down to feed my herbs, shrubs and salads. I've even bought a vacuum shredder for the task, although I seem to spend more time unclogging it than shredding.

As it turns cooler, I find I'm in the kitchen more, experimenting with ingredients and updating classics. Fruit and vegetables that we tend to take for granted, like onions, beetroot and apples, are humble foods that often need just that little extra inspiration to create some interest.

At this time of year freshly dug onions still have all their natural sugars, so they are perfect for lending sweetness to all kinds of savoury dishes and serving as an accompaniment. As a kid, for supper I was often given a bowl of freshly boiled onions from the garden, with melted butter. Gran used to tell me they were good for keeping colds away, which might be true, but I'm sure it was just an excuse to give us some cheap nosh. They tasted good all the same.

I've had some really simple, yet memorable onion dishes around the world. In Tokyo onions are often just sliced and char-grilled, then drizzled with a sweet soy sauce. In Spain the new onions, called calcots, are celebrated for about a month. Typically they are grilled in the open embers of a barbecue and served in pieces of terracotta guttering, with romesco sauce. So maybe we should make them a little more special…

One thing that is changing with some of these modest ingredients is that producers are re-introducing old forgotten varieties. It is not uncommon at farmers' markets these days to find several different types of onions, perhaps four different colours of beetroot, and maybe a dozen or so apple varieties.

Not long ago, beetroot rarely appeared on fashionable menus, but these days it seems to steal the show on the starter

menu in many restaurants. It's as though the boring old beetroot has hopped out of its jar of vinegar and gained culinary status. Now that farmers have started growing old varieties like golden, white and even candy-striped beetroot again, there is plenty of scope for eye-catching dishes. I've unintentionally bluffed dinner guests by serving yellow and white beets in a salad. For all they knew, these could have been swede and turnip until they tasted them.

It is a similar story with apples. Over recent decades, we seem to have neglected the fact that over 3,000 varieties of apples have been grown in this country, each with its own unique flavour. Many traditional apple farmers have lost out to cheaper imports – and the sad fact that their crop was often rejected on the basis that it wasn't consistent in size and shape. But now we seem to be coming round to the fact that apples don't need to be uniform.

Our apple growing history is interesting. Many varieties were brought to us from the Tien Shan mountains on the border of China and Kazakhstan. They arrived via silk traders and the Romans, and where then grafted and cross-pollinated in Victorian times to create new varieties. Some of these have just fallen by the wayside, but many old varieties have been restored recently. You can find them in farmers' markets and good greengrocers across the country. Brogdale Farm in Kent is home to the national fruit collection and houses over 1,800 different apples. Believed to be the most comprehensive collection of apple varieties in the world, it is well worth a visit.

So now you see why simple foods can be of real interest. And of course they are perfect matches to other seasonal ingredients that are around this month – like game and maybe a late running salmon.

Beetroot

Although some of us are still convinced that beetroot only comes in jars of vinegar, there are widespread converts who cook beetroot at home, even if it does take forever. There are many great ways to cook and serve this vegetable, and if you get your hands on some of the old heritage varieties, then all you need is some wild herbs and salad leaves like sorrel or silver sorrel to make a really appetising salad.

Try wrapping red beetroot in foil and baking them for a more intense flavour. Or whiz cooked beetroot to make a vibrant soup and top with freshly grated horseradish. Freshly cooked beetroot tossed in a light dressing is also excellent with cold meats or smoked fish.

BEETROOT SALAD WITH WALNUTS *serves* 4

A simple beetroot salad makes a great light starter for a dinner party salad and it will look stunning if you are able to source different coloured beetroot varieties from a farmers' market or good greengrocer. Cook the different beets separately as their cooking times will vary slightly, also because the red beetroot is likely to stain the others.

500–600g mixed young beetroot (red, golden and white or candy-striped)

salt and freshly ground black pepper

30g good quality shelled walnuts

1 teaspoon good quality sea salt, such as Halen Môn or Maldon

½ tablespoon rapeseed oil

a couple of handfuls of small salad and herb leaves (silver sorrel, red chard, orach, pea shoots, chives, etc.), washed

FOR THE DRESSING

1 tablespoon cider vinegar

1 teaspoon light Suffolk mustard (or similar)

4 tablespoons rapeseed oil

Cook the beetroots separately in salted water for about an hour, depending on the variety and size, until they feel tender when pierced with a sharp knife. Drain and leave until cool enough to handle. Then peel away the skins with your fingers, wearing rubber gloves to stop the red beetroot staining your hands.

Preheat the oven to 180°C/gas 4. Toss the walnuts with the sea salt and rapeseed oil and spread out on a baking tray. Toast in the oven for 4–6 minutes, turning them once or twice, until lightly coloured.

To make the dressing, whisk the ingredients together in a small bowl and season with salt and pepper to taste.

Cut the beetroot into even-sized wedges or halves if they are small. Cut the red ones last so you don't stain the lighter coloured ones.

Arrange the beetroots and salad leaves on plates, season lightly and spoon over the dressing. Scatter over the walnuts and serve.

COLD OX TONGUE WITH BABY BEETS

serves 4

Try to buy fresh young beetroot for this dish – you may need to pre-order them from your greengrocer. Otherwise you could use normal beetroot and cut them into quarters. Cook the ox tongue one or two days in advance if you like, so it is cold and ready to serve. Similarly, you can prepare the beetroot ahead.

1 piece of salted ox tongue, about 800g–1kg

1 onion, peeled and halved

2 carrots, peeled and trimmed

10 black peppercorns

1 bay leaf

1kg young beetroot, cleaned

salt and freshly ground black pepper

2 teaspoons cider vinegar

2 tablespoons rapeseed oil

handful of small salad leaves (red mustard leaf, young beetroot leaves, purslane or red orach)

Put the ox tongue into a large saucepan with the onion, carrots, peppercorns and bay leaf. Bring to the boil, lower the heat and simmer for about 2–2½ hours. Leave to cool in the liquid. While still warm, peel the skin away, using your fingers. You can either keep the tongue as it is, or fit it snugly into a pudding basin or similar mould and put a small plate and weights on top to press it. Either way, refrigerate to set.

Cook the beetroot in their skins in salted water for about 50 minutes to 1 hour, depending on their size. Test with the point of a sharp knife; it should slide in fairly easily once they are cooked. Drain the beetroot and allow them to cool them down a little, then don a pair of rubber gloves and rub off the skins. (If using larger beetroot cut into wedges.) Place in a bowl.

Mix the cider vinegar and rapeseed oil together to make a dressing, season with salt and pepper to taste and pour over the beetroot.

To serve, carve the tongue into thin slices using a sharp knife. Arrange on a large plate or individual ones and pile the beetroot and salad leaves in the centre.

RED MULLET WITH GOLDEN BEETS *serves* 4

This unusual combination works surprisingly well. When I use the more unusual coloured beets, I often find they have more flavour than the familiar red beetroot. Small red mullet are normally very good value for money as restaurant buyers tend to overlook them in favour of larger fish.

300–400g golden beetroot

salt and freshly ground black pepper

800g small red mullet, cleaned and filleted

1 tablespoon rapeseed oil

FOR THE DRESSING

2 small shallots, peeled, halved and finely chopped

1 teaspoon thyme leaves

grated zest of ½ lemon

1 tablespoon cider vinegar

4 tablespoons rapeseed oil

Cook the beetroot in salted water for an hour or until tender when pierced the point of a knife. Leave until cool enough to handle, then remove the skin by rubbing it away with your fingers. Slice the beetroot thinly and arrange on individual plates, to cover most of the plate.

To make the dressing, put the shallots, thyme and lemon zest into a small saucepan with the cider vinegar. Bring to the boil, then take off the heat. Whisk in the rapeseed oil, season with salt and pepper and set aside.

Check the red mullet for pin-bones, removing any you find with tweezers, then season. Heat the rapeseed oil in a large frying pan (preferably non-stick). Lay the fish in the pan, skin side down, and cook over a medium heat for about 2 minutes, then turn and cook for a further minute or so, depending on the size of the fillets.

Remove the pan from the heat and immediately pour the dressing over the fish. Leave to stand for a minute or two, then arrange the red mullet fillets on the beetroot and spoon over the dressing. Serve at once.

Onions

The humble onion is often taken for granted and regarded as a basic kitchen commodity, rather like salt. We rarely serve the vegetable as a dish in its own right, as they do in Spain with the new season calcots (see page 170). With all the different varieties of onions available these days we should be making more of them as a stand-alone vegetable.

Small onions and shallots are great simply roasted in their skins or cooked on the grill or on a ridged griddle pan. Or try puréeing cooked onions with some cream or bèchamel sauce to serve with offal or lamb.

I've never been a great fan of raw onions in dishes, but pickled onions are altogether different – great with cheese, cured and pickled meats, or shredded in salads.

DEEP-FRIED ONIONS IN BEER BATTER

serves 4

I do love deep-fried onions. Rather like deep-fried calamari or scampi in the basket, they are incredibly comforting. A must-have side dish with grilled steak, they could easily replace the chips.

2 white onions, peeled

2 red onions, peeled

1 bunch of spring onions

120g self-raising flour

150–200ml lager to mix

salt and freshly ground black pepper

vegetable or corn oil for frying

plain flour for dusting

onion salt

Cut the white onions into ½cm thick rings; halve the red onions, then cut into ½cm thick slices. Separate into individual rings and slices. Trim the spring onions, but leave whole.

To make the batter, sift the flour into a bowl and whisk in enough of the lager to form a smooth coating batter. Season with salt and pepper to taste.

Heat about an 8cm depth of oil in an electric deep-fat fryer or other suitable heavy-based pan to 160–180°C. Season the flour for dusting well.

You'll need to cook the onions in two or three batches. Toss the first batch in the seasoned flour to coat, shaking off any excess. Now pass the onions through the batter and drop into the hot oil. Deep-fry for about 3–4 minutes until nicely coloured, turning them occasionally with a slotted spoon.

Remove and drain on kitchen paper , then scatter with onion salt. Eat straight away or keep hot while you cook the rest, then serve.

GRILLED OX LIVER WITH CREAMED MUSTARD ONIONS *serves 4*

Being a chef, I've always been obsessed with cooking expensive calf's liver from Holland. I then discovered that ordinary beef liver has similar eating qualities – it doesn't need to be stewed for hours, as our parents and grandparents used to. In fact most offal can cope with brief flash-frying or grilling. You will pay next to nothing for ox liver, as butchers tend to think it has little value.

4 slices of ox liver, each about 120g and ½ cm thick

50g butter

4 large onions, peeled, halved and thinly sliced

salt and freshly ground black pepper

2 teaspoons English mustard

2–3 tablespoons water

4 tablespoons double cream

vegetable oil for brushing

Trim the ox liver, removing any sinews. Melt half the butter in a heavy-based pan, add the onions and cook gently with the lid on for about 8–10 minutes until they are really soft, stirring every so often. Season with salt and pepper and stir in the mustard. Add the water and simmer until it has evaporated. Pour in the double cream and let it simmer very gently, stirring every so often, until it just binds the onions. Cover with a lid and keep warm.

Heat a ridged griddle pan until it is almost smoking. Season the liver with salt and pepper and brush with oil. Griddle for about 30 seconds on each side so that it stays nice and pink, then serve on the creamed onions.

VARIATIONS Creamed onions are a great accompaniment to other offal, such as lamb's or calf's kidneys, as well as simply grilled steaks. They are also good with salt beef.

BEEF FLANK, CRISPY SHALLOT AND WATERCRESS SALAD *serves 4*

This was something I concocted at home one night because there was only one steak in the fridge and the best way to stretch it to feed two was in a salad. I love the idea of a main course salad at any time of the year – it's light enough for a lunch or late supper, and you can almost invent a new one every night. I've used 'butcher's steak' here (described in more detail on page 205). It is probably the tastiest cut you can buy – and one of the least expensive.

2 butcher's steaks, each about 300g (or larger if you wish)

salt and freshly ground black pepper

100–150g watercress, trimmed and thick stalks removed

FOR THE CRISPY SHALLOTS
5–6 shallots, peeled

vegetable oil for deep-frying

plain flour for dusting

100ml milk

FOR THE DRESSING
1 tablespoon good quality cider vinegar

3 tablespoons extra virgin rapeseed oil

1 teaspoon English mustard (preferably Tewksbury)

Trim the steaks of any excess fat and set them aside at room temperature.

Slice the shallots into thin rings. Heat about an 8cm depth of oil in an electric deep-fat fryer or other suitable heavy-based pan to 160–180°C. Season the flour for dusting generously with salt and pepper.

Toss the shallot rings in the seasoned flour to coat, shaking off any excess, then pass through the milk and then through the flour again shaking off excess. Deep-fry the shallot rings a handful at a time for 3–4 minutes until crisp, then remove with a slotted spoon and drain on kitchen paper. Repeat with the rest (you don't need to worry about keeping the onions hot).

Heat a ridged griddle pan or a heavy-based frying pan, or better still a barbecue. Season the steaks well and cook to your liking. Allow about 3–4 minutes on each side for rare to medium-rare, which I'd recommend, especially for a salad.

Meanwhile, make the dressing. Whisk the ingredients together in a bowl and season with salt and pepper to taste. Dress the watercress and arrange on serving plates. Slice the steaks and arrange on the watercress, then scatter the crispy shallots on top and serve.

Apples

Our apple heritage is second to none and the apple orchards of Kent are thought to be the best in the world. Old established varieties lend themselves to all manner of great dishes. From rustic tarts, pies and crumbles to sauces and chutneys, apples are the good old year-round standby. A childhood favourite of mine is deep-fried apple rings served with clotted cream ... pure indulgence.

Apple sauce, made with tart Bramley cooking apples is the perfect partner to roast pork, duck and goose, as its slight acidity cuts the richness. To make it, simply peel, core and roughly chop 1kg Bramley's and cook with a couple of tablespoonfuls of caster sugar and a knob of butter until the apples start to break down. Serve the sauce chunky or purée in a blender if you prefer.

MUSSELS COOKED IN SOMERSET CIDER
serves 4

With their plump, juicy flesh, mussels are at their peak at this time of the year. We are all so conditioned to pouring wine into our sauces that we tend to forget about using our native drinks instead. Both cider and beer are great for cooking mussels.

2kg fresh mussels

a good knob of butter

1 small onion, peeled, halved and finely chopped

2 garlic cloves, peeled and crushed

6 rashers of good quality streaky bacon, derinded and finely chopped

400ml Somerset dry cider

100ml double cream

2 tablespoons finely chopped parsley

salt and freshly ground black pepper

Scrub the mussels thoroughly and remove the beards. Discard any with open shells that do not close when sharply tapped.

Melt the butter in a cooking pot large enough to hold the mussels. Add the onion, garlic and bacon and cook gently for 3–4 minutes to soften the onion. Add the cider and simmer for a minute or so. Add the mussels, cover with a tight-fitting lid and cook over a high heat for 3–4 minutes, shaking the pan frequently and giving them an occasional stir.

Drain the mussels in a colander over a bowl to catch the liquor. Return this to the pan and stir in the cream and chopped parsley. Bring to the boil and season with salt and pepper to taste. Meanwhile, divide the mussels among warm bowls, discarding any that have not opened. Pour over the liquor.

Serve immediately, with some good rustic bread for mopping up the juices, remembering to provide spare bowls for the discarded shells.

GLOUCESTERSHIRE OLD SPOT PORK AND BLENHEIM ORANGE APPLE PIE

makes 1 large pie or 6 small pies

Homemade pies are so much better than shop-bought ones and you can bespoke the filling to suit what's in season. Don't be put off if you haven't got a mincer at home – just chop the meat up very finely by hand, or ask a helpful butcher to mince it for you. I used Blenheim orange apples, which I scrumped from Simon Kelner's back garden right next to Blenheim palace, but you could use any other flavourful seasonal apple. The pastry is easy to prepare.

You can either make the pie in an old-fashioned rectangular raised pie mould as I've done, or shape them by hand like a traditional pork pie. I quite like to eat this pie warm as it brings out the flavours in the filling and the pastry tends to be crisper, but I've included a method for jellying the pie(s) to serve cold if you prefer.

FOR THE HOT WATER CRUST PASTRY

500g plain flour, plus extra for dusting

½ teaspoon salt

200ml water

175g lard

1 egg, beaten, to glaze

FOR THE FILLING

400g minced pork (about 30% fat, such as from the belly)

1 teaspoon chopped thyme leaves

grated zest of 2 oranges

salt and freshly ground black pepper

3–4 Blenheim orange apples (or another tasty variety)

FOR THE JELLY

2 sheets of leaf gelatine

150ml chicken stock

To make the pastry, mix the flour and salt together in a bowl and make a well in the centre. Bring the water and lard to the boil in a pan, then pour into the flour well and stir with a wooden spoon to form a smooth dough. Cover the dough with a cloth and leave for about 15 minutes until it is cool enough to handle.

Preheat the oven to 200°C/gas 6. For the filling, in a bowl, mix the minced pork together with the thyme and orange zest. Season well. Peel, core and slice the apples.

If you are using a large pie mould (or perhaps two smaller moulds), roll out two-thirds of the pastry on a lightly floured surface and use to line the mould(s). Layer the pork mixture in the mould(s) alternating with one or two layers of apple slices. Roll out the rest of the pastry to make pie lid(s). Lay on top of the pie(s) and press the pastry edges together with your fingers to seal. If you intend to serve them cold (with jelly), cut a 1cm hole in the centre of the pastry lid.

If you are making individual pork pies, roll out a ball of dough on a lightly floured surface to a 12–14cm diameter. Roll out another round, about half the size, for the top. Spoon some of the pork filling into the centre of the larger round and put a few apple slices in the middle. Lay the smaller round on top. Now raise the sides of the larger round up to meet the lid and pinch the edges together with your fingers. If it looks a bit misshapen, you can reshape it as the pastry is quite pliable. Repeat to make another five individual pies.

Brush the pie(s) all over with the beaten egg and bake until a skewer inserted in the centre feels hot when you remove it – allow 35–40 minutes for individual pies; 50–55 minutes for larger pies. If the pie(s) appear to be colouring too quickly, cover loosely with foil and turn the oven down slightly.

Place the cooked pie(s) on a wire rack. If serving warm, leave to stand for 5–10 minutes.

If serving cold, allow the pie(s) to cool, then chill overnight. The following day, soak the gelatine leaves in cold water to cover for a few minutes. Meanwhile, bring the stock to a simmer. Remove the stock from the heat, squeeze the gelatine leaves to remove excess water, then add to the hot stock and stir until fully dissolved. Leave to cool, but do not let it set. Pour the jelly into the pies to reach the top and return to the fridge to set.

To serve, carefully remove the pie(s) from the moulds if using. Serve warm or cold, ideally with homemade piccalilli (see page 15) or redcurrant jelly if you prefer.

SPICED PARSNIP AND APPLE SOUP

serves 4–6

Parsnips make a hearty, sweet soup – ideal when the weather begins to get a bit chilly. Teamed with apples like Russets or Cox's and mild background spices, they are amazingly good. This is a mildly curried soup; increase the quantities of spices if you want it to be more fiery.

2–3 large Russet or Cox's apples,
400–500g in total

500g parsnips

60g butter

1 teaspoon chopped fresh root ginger

1 teaspoon ground cumin

½ teaspoon ground cinnamon

1 teaspoon fenugreek seeds

½ teaspoon ground turmeric

100ml cider

about 1½ litres vegetable stock

salt and freshly ground black pepper

90ml double cream

2 teaspoons toasted cumin seeds, to finish

Peel, core and roughly dice the apples and parsnips. Melt the butter in a large saucepan, tip in the diced parsnips and apples, then add the fresh ginger and spices. Cover and cook gently for about 5 minutes, giving them an occasional stir; don't let them colour.

Remove the lid, add the cider and vegetable stock and bring to the boil. Season with salt and pepper and simmer gently for about 15 minutes until the parsnip is soft.

Purée the soup in a blender until smooth, then strain through a fine sieve back into the cleaned pan. Bring back to a low simmer, then stir in the cream. If the soup is too thick, adjust the consistency with a little water or additional stock.

Divide between warm soup bowls and sprinkle with a pinch of cumin seeds to serve.

APPLE AND COBNUT TART *serves 4–6*

Bramley apples cook down to a well-flavoured purée, which makes a perfect filling for this autumnal tart, especially if you spike it with a little apple brandy. The crunchy, nutty crumble topping provides a good contrast. Best served with Devonshire clotted cream.

FOR THE PASTRY

2 medium egg yolks

225g unsalted butter, softened, plus extra for greasing

1 tablespoon caster sugar

275g plain flour, plus extra for dusting

FOR THE FILLING

3 large Bramley apples

30g unsalted butter

2 tablespoons Somerset apple brandy

75g caster sugar

FOR THE CRUMBLE TOPPING

80g plain flour

40g unsalted butter, diced small

60g caster sugar

20 or so cobnuts, shelled and chopped

First make the pastry. Beat the egg yolks and butter together in a bowl until evenly blended, then beat in the sugar. Stir in the flour and knead together until well mixed. Gather the pastry into a ball, wrap in cling film and leave to rest in the fridge for an hour.

Lightly butter a 26cm tart tin or 4 individual ones. Roll out the pastry on a lightly floured surface to a ½cm thickness and use to line the tin(s). Trim the edges and refrigerate for 1 hour.

Meanwhile, for the filling, peel, core and roughly chop the apples. Melt the butter in a pan, tip in the apples and cook for 4–5 minutes until soft. Add the apple brandy and sugar, stir well until dissolved, then remove from the heat.

To make the crumble, briefly whiz the flour, butter and sugar together in a food processor or mixer until the mixture resembles coarse breadcrumbs, or place in a bowl and rub together with your fingertips. Fold in the chopped nuts.

Preheat the oven to 190°C/gas 5. Line the tart(s) with greaseproof paper, fill with a layer of baking beans and bake blind for 10–15 minutes until the pastry is light golden. Lower the oven setting to 180°C/gas 4. Remove the beans and paper and fill the case with the warm apple mixture. Scatter the crumble over the top and bake for 20–30 minutes until the topping is golden brown. Serve with clotted cream.

APPLE CHUTNEY *makes about 1.5–2kg*

This is an easy chutney to make and you can modify it to suit your own taste. Any variety of dessert apple will do, as the strong flavouring ingredients will take over the nuance of the apple. They will, however, need to be firm and very fresh. Serve with cheese, cold ham or tongue, or cold pork pies.

2kg firm, ripe dessert apples

550ml cider vinegar

450g soft brown sugar

100g salt

30g black mustard seeds

20g peeled fresh root ginger, grated

a good pinch of cayenne pepper

Peel, core and chop the apples roughly into 1cm chunks. Put into a heavy-based saucepan with all of the other ingredients and bring slowly to the boil, stirring occasionally to encourage the sugar to dissolve.

Simmer for about 30–40 minutes until the apples are disintegrating, then remove from the heat. The liquid should be thick and syrupy by now. If not, strain it into another pan and boil to reduce down and thicken, then pour back over the apples.

Tip into a clean bowl, cover and leave to stand in a cool place for 2–3 days, stirring every so often. Then transfer to sterilised Kilner or other preserving jars, seal with vinegar-proof lids and store in a cool place. Refrigerate once opened and use within 3–4 weeks.

November

Old English MUTTON, *tasty* BEEF BITS, *natural* smoked HADDOCK *and beautiful* winter chanterelles – *the pick of the wild mushrooms now...*

OTHER INGREDIENTS NOT TO BE MISSED

Sprats   Pike   Herring   Bass   Mussels   Partridge   Pheasant   Wild duck   Teal   Snipe   Woodcock

Parsnips   Swede   Jerusalem artichokes   Brussels sprouts and sprout tops   Red cabbage   Savoy cabbage   Pumpkins

Squashes   Salsify   Leeks   Burdock root   Watercress   Dittander   Toad flax

Ceps   Charcoal burners   Puffball   Hedgehog fungus   Horn of plenty   Wood blewets

Rosehips   Apples   Quince   Pears   Crab apples

November is the time to turn to winter warmers that you look forward to coming home to. I like to use unusual cuts of meat at this time of the year that often get forgotten about, or that butchers don't stock on their shelves, unless you really twist their arm to do so. These cuts are often the tastiest but need a little more skill and attention to prepare and cook. Mutton, for example, is starting to become appreciated again. It is perfect for slow cooking and once braised its flavour will surpass that of any cut of lamb. The revival has been a struggle

and as a part of the mutton renaissance I'm doing my bit to convince the general public that it's much more than just an old sheep. From October through till spring, this tasty meat should be on our shopping lists.

Similarly, there are lots of cuts of beef that call for long, slow cooking, which get left by the wayside in our modern day 'no time to spend hours in the kitchen' lifestyles. A carcass of beef holds many surprises tucked away next to prime cuts and in among less obvious parts of the animal. Elsewhere in Europe, these cuts are commonly used – it's just that our butchers haven't got the demand for them, so they are more likely to end up in the mincer. We really are missing out on some of the tastiest meat. It's just a case of getting our heads around using them – and realising that slow cooking is effortless. All that's needed is a bit of forethought to assemble the dish, then it can be left to cook alone. Alternatively, if you want to speed things up a bit, you can use a pressure cooker to cut down the cooking time - and save energy too.

On the fishy front, I have chosen to feature haddock this month. It is one of the

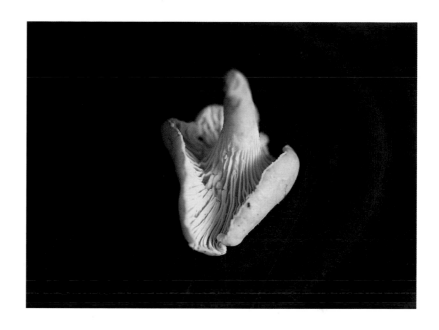

better-known fish that seems to be surviving the sustainability factor a bit better than many common species, including its cousin the cod. I guess haddock is less fashionable on restaurant menus and not so easy to sell, except on fish and chip shop menus that is. In its smoked form, it has always been popular, appearing on breakfast menus, in the form of Arbroath smokies and Finnan haddock. Whatever you buy in the way of smoked haddock, do avoid that brightly coloured dyed stuff. It isn't even appealing to the eye and doesn't taste nearly as good as naturally smoked fish.

Winter chanterelles are perfect for gathering now. They are one of those fungi that thrive in cold conditions and will still show their caps through several frosts - I've often picked them right through till mid-December. Also, because they are so light, a hard-picked kilo will go a long way and certainly stay within the legal quantity for Epping forest officials.

These chanterelles are the most delicate of all the fungi and should ideally be picked when it is dry, certainly not after a downpour, otherwise when you cook them you'll find the pan just fills with water and you end up with boiled mushrooms. They are perfect with game at this time of the year, and I like to throw a handful into a pan with a fried egg for breakfast.

This is also a great time of the year to make chutneys and jellies with quince, apples and crab apples, and to pickle some vegetables to last you through the winter. Pickled red cabbage, which is excellent right now, is delicious with hotpots and wintry stews, or simply with cold leftover meats.

Haddock

Haddock has very similar eating qualities to cod and can be treated in exactly the same way: dipped in batter, deep-fried and served with a pea purée or mushy peas; pan-fried in butter and served with parsley sauce or sea vegetables; or poached, flaked and combined with smoked haddock and salmon in a creamy sauce and baked under a potato crust for a comforting fish pie.

Smoked haddock makes a great alternative to the great British fry-up and offers lots of possibilities for breakfast or brunch. You can simply serve it topped with a poached egg, transform it into kedgeree or turn it into a hash-like fish cake with a fried egg on top. One of my favourite smoked haddock dishes, though, is Cullen skink – a comforting Scottish soup. Just make sure you use natural, undyed smoked haddock.

CREAMED ARBROATH SMOKIES WITH SOFT-BOILED DUCK'S EGG *serves* 4

Arbroath smokies are not as popular as they once were and are due for a bit of a revival in my view. Along with kippers, they've just drifted out of vogue – perhaps because the smell of them cooking was too much, or maybe the bones were off-putting. I'd say they are definitely worth cooking, as their flavour is sublime. If you can't get Arbroath smokies, then just poach and lightly flake some smoked Finnan haddock. Serve with toast soldiers as a breakfast dish or a starter.

2 Arbroath smokies, skinned and boned, or about 500g smoked haddock fillet, skinned

milk for poaching (if using smoked haddock)

a couple of good knobs of butter

1 leek, halved, finely shredded and washed

250–300ml double cream

salt and freshly ground black pepper

4 duck's eggs

1 tablespoon chopped parsley

Check the fish carefully for any pin-bones, removing any you find with tweezers. If using smoked haddock, poach it in gently simmering milk or water to cover for 3–4 minutes, then drain and break up the flesh into fairly large pieces.

Heat the butter in a pan and gently cook the leek for 3–4 minutes until soft, then add the cream and fish. Season lightly and simmer until the cream has reduced down and is just coating the fish. Taste and adjust the seasoning if necessary.

Meanwhile, soft-boil the duck's eggs by carefully lowering them into a pan of simmering water and cooking gently for 5 minutes. Briefly refresh in cold water until the eggs are cool enough to handle, then remove and carefully peel.

Divide the creamed fish and leek among warm plates and sprinkle with the chopped parsley. Carefully cut the soft-boiled duck's eggs in half and place one on each serving. Grind over a little pepper and serve at once.

HADDOCK FISH FINGERS *serves 4*

These might be a bit more labour-intensive than reaching into the freezer for a packet of fish fingers, but they are far superior and well worth the extra effort. Kids love them, of course, but grown-ups do too, especially if you serve them with tartare sauce and classic mushy peas, or a simple salad and chips. I often serve them with a posh pea purée – made by simply blending a bag of frozen peas to a coarse purée. You can use pollack or any other firm white fish in place of haddock.

    500g haddock fillet, skinned

    salt and freshly ground black pepper

    plain flour for dusting

    1 large egg, beaten

    100g fresh white breadcrumbs

    vegetable or corn oil for frying

Cut the haddock fillet into 8cm x 2cm fingers and season with salt and pepper. Put the flour in one shallow dish, the beaten egg in another and the breadcrumbs in a third dish. One at a time, dip each piece of fish first into the flour, then in the beaten egg and finally into the breadcrumbs to coat all over.

Heat a thin film of oil in a heavy-based frying pan and cook the fish fingers for about 2 minutes on each side until nicely browned.

Drain on kitchen paper and serve straight away, with ketchup and pea purée if you like.

KEDGEREE *serves 4*

Originally known as *khichri*, this Hindi dish has come a long way since its creation by the British in India all those years ago. It is an excellent way to use up fish and rice, but as always, good quality ingredients are crucial even in a dish made primarily from leftovers. Smoked Finnan haddock makes the best kedgeree by far, as the smokiness travels through the sauce and rice to give that delicious savoury flavour.

I sometimes replace a little of the haddock with hot smoked salmon fillet (braden rost) or smoked mackerel, for a contrast in colour and flavour.

    350g undyed smoked haddock fillet

    150g basmati rice

    salt and freshly ground black pepper

    1 teaspoon cumin seeds

    1 teaspoon onion (nigella) seeds

    4 medium eggs

FOR THE CURRY SAUCE

    a couple of good knobs of butter

    2 shallots, peeled and finely chopped

    1 garlic clove, peeled and crushed

    a small piece of fresh root ginger, peeled and grated

    ¼ teaspoon ground turmeric

    ¼ teaspoon ground cumin

    ½ teaspoon curry powder

    ½ teaspoon fennel seeds

    a few curry leaves

    a pinch of saffron threads

    2 teaspoons plain flour

    100ml fish stock (or ¼ good stock cube dissolved in this amount of hot water)

    250ml double cream

First make the curry sauce. Melt the butter in a heavy-based pan and add the shallots, garlic and ginger. Cook gently to soften the shallots, without allowing them to colour. Add all the spices and cook for another minute to release their flavours. Stir in the flour, then slowly add the fish stock, stirring constantly to avoid lumps forming.

Bring to the boil and let bubble to reduce by half. Pour in the cream and simmer until reduced by half again. Whiz the sauce in a blender, or using a hand-held stick blender until smooth, then strain it through a fine-meshed sieve. Season with salt and pepper to taste.

Poach the smoked haddock in a shallow pan of gently simmering water for 3–4 minutes. Remove from the heat and leave the fish to cool in the liquor.

Rinse the rice a couple of times in cold water to remove excess starch, then cook in plenty of boiling salted water with the cumin and onion seeds for about 12–15 minutes until just cooked. Briefly drain it in a colander, then return to the pan, put the lid back on and leave off the heat for a few minutes. This allows the rice to steam dry and gives it a nice light fluffy texture.

In the meantime, soft-boil the eggs in a pan of simmering water for 4 minutes, then drain and run under the cold tap for a minute until cool enough to handle.

To serve the kedgeree, reheat the sauce and add the cooked smoked haddock. Peel the eggs and carefully cut each one in half. Divide the rice among warm bowls, spoon over the fish and sauce, then place a soft-boiled egg on each portion. Serve at once.

Winter chanterelles

These beautiful yellow mushrooms have an exquisite texture and are probably the most versatile of all wild fungi as they have so many uses in cooking. Perfect partners for game, beef and duck, they are also great simply scattered onto pan-fried fish with lots of chopped parsley and a squeeze of lemon.

Serve them on toast for a fast snack, or scattered over a fried egg for a perfect start to the morning. And of course, you can sauté them quickly and add them at the last minute to risottos, pasta dishes, even pizzas.

However you intend to cook them, don't be tempted to wash chanterelles, otherwise they will absorb the water and simply boil once they hit the pan, ruining their delicate texture. Instead, just cut away any soil or moss and brush away any dirt, using a soft mushroom brush.

You also need to be careful not to overcook these mushrooms. They will cook really quickly in a smoking hot pan with foaming butter – a minute is almost too long, so watch them carefully and remove from the heat the moment they are ready.

MONKFISH CHEEK AND CHANTERELLE SALAD *serves 4 as a starter*

Monkfish cheeks are not commonly seen on fishmonger's slabs and you'll probably need to pre-order them. Using these types of cuts is certainly the way forward to helping the sustainability problem; mind you the fisherman whose task it is to cut them out might well disagree with me.

You can treat both monkfish and skate cheeks in the same way as any cut of fish, except that they have the added advantage of responding well to a bit of slow cooking – in a stew, curry or fish soup, for example. They also freeze well, so it's worth ordering extra to store in the freezer in small, usable batches.

2 handfuls of watercress or other small winter salad leaves

12–15 monkfish cheeks, about 200–250g in total

salt and freshly ground black pepper

60–70g butter

150g chanterelles, cleaned

FOR THE DRESSING

1 tablespoon cider vinegar

juice of ½ lemon

1 teaspoon mustard, such as Tewksbury

4–5 tablespoons extra virgin rapeseed oil

For the dressing, whisk all the ingredients together in a bowl and season with salt and pepper; set aside.

Wash the salad leaves, trim and pat dry, then arrange on individual serving plates.

Season the monkfish cheeks and cut them in half if they are large. Heat half of the butter in a heavy-based frying pan until foaming and cook the monkfish cheeks for 4–5 minutes, turning them until nicely coloured all over. Remove to a plate and keep warm. Wipe out the pan.

Add the rest of the butter to the pan and heat until foaming, then add the chanterelles, season and cook for about 30–40 seconds, turning every so often.

Arrange the warm monkfish cheeks on the salad leaves and spoon over the dressing. Spoon the chanterelles on top and serve immediately.

PHEASANT, CHESTNUT AND CHANTERELLE SOUP *serves 6–8*

I must confess that pheasant is probably my least favourite of the game birds. It has a tendency to dry out in the oven before you know it and can be very disappointing. It must either be timed to perfection or slow cooked. Using pheasant in a soup like this, however, gets around the problem – and one bird goes a long way. You can prepare the soup base, roast the chestnuts and get everything together the day before, ready to reheat and assemble everything just before serving.

1 oven-ready pheasant

1 onion, peeled and roughly chopped

1 small leek, roughly chopped and washed

a few sprigs of thyme

2 litres chicken stock (or 2 good stock cubes dissolved in the same amount of hot water)

a glass of white wine

salt and freshly ground black pepper

40g butter

30g plain flour

16–18 fresh chestnuts in the shell

2–3 tablespoons double cream

150g chanterelles, cleaned

2 tablespoons chopped parsley

Cut the legs from the pheasant using a sharp knife, then carefully remove the breasts. Place the legs, breasts and carcass in a cooking pot with the onion, leek, thyme, chicken stock and wine. Season lightly, bring to the boil, then lower the heat and simmer gently for 10 minutes.

Take out the pheasant breasts and set aside on a plate. Continue to simmer the soup for a further 20 minutes. Melt the butter in a small saucepan and stir in the flour over a low heat. Whisk the flour and butter mixture into the simmering soup in pieces to thicken it, then continue to simmer for another 20 minutes.

Meanwhile, preheat the oven to 200°C/gas 6. Score the chestnuts and place on a small baking tray. Cover with foil and bake for about 12–15 minutes, then remove to a plate and leave until cool enough to handle. Peel away the skins and cut each chestnut into two or three pieces.

Strain the soup through a fine sieve into a clean saucepan and add the cream. Remove the pheasant meat from the legs and cut the breast into bite-sized pieces. Add to the soup with the chestnuts, chanterelles and chopped parsley. Simmer gently for 5 minutes. Check the seasoning and serve.

GOOSNARGH DUCK WITH CREAMED SPINACH AND CHANTERELLES *serves 4*

There are more and more good poultry farms in the UK now, but the ducks Reg Johnson's farms in Goosnargh up in Lancashire are still my favourite. They have just the right amount of fat covering and perfectly tender, well-flavoured flesh.

2 oven-ready ducks, preferably Goosnargh

salt and freshly ground black pepper

a couple of knobs of butter

200g chanterelles, cleaned

2 tablespoons chopped parsley

FOR THE CREAMED SPINACH

400–500g spinach, stalks removed, washed

200ml double cream

a good pinch of freshly grated nutmeg

Preheat the oven to 230°C/gas 8. Season the ducks inside and out, then place in a roasting tray and roast for 20 minutes. Lower the oven setting to 200°C/gas 6 and continue cooking for another 15 minutes, basting every so often. Remove the ducks from the tray, leave to cool a little, then cut off the legs. Return the legs to the oven and cook them for another 30 minutes, basting and turning every so often.

Meanwhile, bring a pan of well-salted water to the boil. Add the spinach and cook for 2–3 minutes. Drain in a colander, pressing out any excess water with a plate.

Put the spinach into a pan with the cream and stir for a minute, then whiz to a coarse purée in a food processor. Return to the pan and simmer until the purée has reduced and thickened. Season with salt, pepper and nutmeg to taste; keep warm.

Reheat the duck (including the legs) in the oven for about 10 minutes. Meanwhile, melt the butter in a large heavy-based frying pan and heat until foaming. You may need to cook the chanterelles in two batches. Add them to the pan, season and scatter over the parsley. Cook over a high heat for about 30–40 seconds, turning them every so often, then remove from the heat.

To serve, cut the breasts from the ducks with a sharp knife and halve them. Spoon the creamed spinach onto warm serving plates and arrange the duck breasts and legs on top. Spoon the chanterelles over and serve.

CREAMED SPINACH AND CHANTERELLES
serves 4–6

Spinach and chanterelles, with their rustic flavours, lend themselves to a little indulgence of cream. This is a perfect side dish for meat, fish and game, or you can simply serve it as a starter with a poached free-range hen's or duck's egg on top.

500g spinach, large stalks removed
a couple of good knobs of butter
150–200g chanterelles, cleaned
salt and freshly ground black pepper
150ml double cream

Wash the spinach well and dry in a salad spinner or pat dry with a tea towel. Heat half of the butter in a large saucepan and cook the spinach over a high heat, stirring it every so often, for 3–4 minutes until it is wilted and tender. Tip into a colander and leave to drain.

Heat the rest of the butter in the same pan. Add the chanterelles and fry briefly for a minute, seasoning them lightly with salt and pepper and turning them to colour evenly as they cook.

Pour in the cream and let bubble until reduced by about two-thirds and thickened, then stir in the spinach. Cook over a medium heat for a minute or two and re-season if necessary. Serve straight away.

WHIPPED POTATOES WITH CHANTERELLES *serves 4 as a starter*

Two simple earthy ingredients – potatoes and wild mushrooms – come together to make a perfect dinner party starter. The secret here is to be very generous with the butter in the whipped potatoes so they almost become sauce-like, and of course you don't need very much of them. Chanterelles look particularly attractive, but you can use ceps, hedgehog fungus or girolles – whatever you can lay your hands on.

300–400g waxy potatoes, such as Charlotte or Anya
salt and freshly ground black pepper
250g butter, cut into small pieces
100ml double cream
150–200g chanterelles, cleaned
1 tablespoon chopped parsley

Peel the potatoes and cook in boiling salted water until tender. Drain and mash finely – ideally using a potato ricer. If you use a masher, then push them through a sieve afterwards.

Put the potato into a pan with 200g of the butter, season with salt and pepper and stir over a low heat until the butter has melted. Add the cream, re-season if necessary and keep warm.

Melt the remaining butter in a large heavy-based frying pan and heat until foaming. You may need to cook the chanterelles in two batches. Drop them into the pan with the parsley, season and cook over a high heat for a minute or so, turning every so often.

To serve, spoon the whipped potato in a thin layer on each warm plate and scatter the chanterelles over the top. Serve at once.

Mutton

It has been, and still is, a bit of a struggle to convince the general public that mutton is far superior to lamb for long, slow cooking. It has a superb depth of flavour and is perfect for casseroles, hotpots and flavoursome meaty broths. You can also slow-roast certain cuts, such as leg and shoulder. Just ask your butcher to order some in for you if he doesn't stock mutton on a regular basis.

Some cuts – like the best end – can be treated in the same way as lamb. The recipe for fried breaded cutlets (on page 82), for example, works just as well with mutton. For most cuts though, think in terms of slow gentle cooking and you will be impressed with the results.

MUTTON BROTH *serves* 4

Long, slow cooking not only suits mutton, it also gives you a well-flavoured stock to make the broth. You can vary the vegetables and pulses here, according to what you have in your fridge and larder – perhaps adding yellow or green split peas, maple peas, celeriac or any other root vegetable. Even a few cabbage leaves at the end would add a touch of colour and texture.

200g neck of mutton fillet

½ teaspoon chopped thyme leaves

1 onion, peeled and finely chopped

2 litres lamb or chicken stock (or 2 good stock cubes dissolved in this amount of hot water)

salt and freshly ground black pepper

30g pearl barley

1 medium carrot

1 medium parsnip

100–120g swede

1 small turnip

1 tablespoon chopped parsley

Cut the mutton roughly into 1cm dice and put into a large heavy-based pan with the thyme leaves and onion. Pour on the stock to cover and season with salt and pepper. Bring to the boil, then lower the heat, cover and simmer very gently for about an hour until the mutton is tender.

In the meantime, soak the pearl barley in cold water to cover for an hour. Peel all the root vegetables and cut into rough ½cm cubes. Drain the pearl barley and add to the broth with the vegetables. Simmer for another 30 minutes.

Add the chopped parsley and simmer for a further 10 minutes. Taste and adjust the seasoning, then ladle into warm soup plates and serve.

MUTTON AND TURNIP HOTPOT *serves 4–6*

This is basically a Lancashire hotpot, incorporating turnips as well as potatoes. There are various versions of this traditional dish, but the main ingredient is usually a flavoursome cut of lamb, such as the neck, which is traditionally cut on the bone like chops. I prefer to use mutton, as the end flavour is far better – almost gamey. Kidneys and black pudding are sometimes added to a classic hotpot and, back in the days when they were cheap, a few oysters would have been put under the potato topping near the end of cooking.

1–1.5kg mutton neck chops

salt and freshly ground black pepper

plain flour for dusting

6 lamb's kidneys, halved and trimmed (optional)

4–5 tablespoons vegetable oil

450–500g onions, peeled and thinly sliced

60g unsalted butter, plus exta, melted, for brushing

800ml lamb or beef stock

1 teaspoon chopped rosemary leaves

500g large potatoes

500g large turnips

Preheat the oven to 220°C/gas 7. Season the mutton chops with salt and pepper and dust with flour. Do the same with the kidneys if you're including them. Heat a heavy-based frying pan and add 2 tablespoons oil. Fry the chops, a few at a time, over a high heat until nicely coloured, then remove to a colander to drain. If using kidneys, fry them briefly to colour; drain and set aside.

Wipe out the pan, then add another 2 tablespoons of oil and fry the onions over a high heat until they begin to colour. Add the butter and continue to cook for a few minutes until they soften. Dust the onions with a tablespoonful of flour, stir well, then gradually add the stock, stirring to avoid lumps. Sprinkle in the chopped rosemary. Bring to the boil, season with salt and pepper, then lower the heat and simmer for about 10 minutes. Peel the potatoes and turnips and cut into 3mm slices.

To assemble, take a deep casserole dish with lid. Cover the bottom with a layer of potatoes and turnips followed by a layer of meat moistened with a little sauce, then another layer of potatoes and turnips. Continue in this way until the meat and most of the sauce have been used, ending with turnips and finally an overlapping layer of potato slices. Brush the top with a little of the sauce.

Cover and cook in the hot oven for about 30 minutes. Now turn the oven down to 140°C/gas 1 and cook slowly for a further 2 hours or until the meat is tender.

Remove the lid and turn the oven back up to 220°C/gas 7. Brush the potato topping with a little melted butter and return to the oven for 15 minutes or so to allow the potatoes to brown.

Beef bits

I'm keen to encourage everyone to think beyond the prime cuts and cook with the less popular 'secondary cuts'. Many of these are much tastier too; it's just that most of them call for long, slow cooking. Ox cheeks, oxtail, beef short ribs, shin and flank all have a great flavour and are perfect for braising. Serve as warming winter casseroles or turn into pies, and if you have any

leftovers, use them to make interesting winter salads. Butcher's steak is a great inexpensive alternative to rump or sirloin steak and can be cooked in a similar fashion.

BUTCHER'S STEAK WITH BONE MARROW AND WILD MUSHROOMS *serves* 4

This cut is highly regarded in France, where it is known as *onglet*. In the US it is called hanger steak and you see it on most decent brasserie menus. Here, it is more likely to get used as stewing steak than cooked as a proper steak. Old school butchers knew how good it was, though, saving it for themselves once the beast was butchered – hence the name. It lies just below the kidneys, near the flank and has a wonderful flavour. You'll probably need to order the meat in advance from your butcher; you'll also need to ask him to saw the bone marrow shaft in half lengthways.

    4 butcher's steaks, each about 200g
    2 x 8cm lengths of bone marrow, halved
    lengthways
    a couple of good knobs of butter
    4 small shallots, peeled and finely
    chopped
    2 garlic cloves, peeled and crushed
    50–60g fresh white breadcrumbs
    2 tablespoons chopped parsley
    salt and freshly ground black pepper
    1 tablespoon vegetable oil for brushing
    120–150g wild mushrooms, such as winter
    chanterelles

Set the butcher's steaks aside on a plate to bring them to room temperature. Preheat the oven to 200°C/gas 6.

To prepare the bone marrow, heat a little of the butter in a pan and gently cook the shallots and garlic for 2–3 minutes until softened, then remove from the heat. Scoop the bone marrow out of the bones with a spoon and chop roughly. Toss with the shallot mix, breadcrumbs, chopped parsley and some seasoning. Spoon the mixture back into the bones, place on a baking tray and bake in the oven for about 12–15 minutes until lightly coloured.

Meanwhile, heat a ridged griddle pan or heavy-based frying pan. Season the steaks, lightly oil them and cook in the hot pan for about 3–4 minutes on each side, keeping them fairly rare, then set aside to rest in a warm place.

Meanwhile, heat the rest of the butter in a heavy-based frying pan until foaming. Add the chanterelles, season and cook over a high heat for just 30 seconds. (More meaty wild mushrooms will take longer; allow a few minutes.)

To serve, cut each steak into about 5 slices and arrange on warm plates with the stuffed bone marrow alongside. Spoon the mushrooms over the steaks and serve.

BRAISED SHORT RIBS WITH INNIS AND GUNN *serves* 4

This cut, sometimes called Jacob's ladder because of its appearance, is a by-product of the Sunday rib roast. The short ribs usually get sawn off, then stripped of their meat for mince and discarded, or sold to chefs for the stockpot. Between the ribs are some of the tastiest morsels on the beast – perfect for braises where cuts such as flank, brisket or shin would normally be used. Your butcher may have some to hand, but if not, ask him to save you some.

2kg beef short ribs, cut to about 10cm in length, then cut through the bones

salt and freshly ground black pepper

2 tablespoons plain flour

2 onions, peeled and roughly chopped

2 celery sticks, roughly chopped

1 carrot, peeled and roughly chopped

1 tsp tomato purée

330ml bottle Innis and Gunn beer

2 litres beef stock

3 garlic cloves, peeled and chopped

1 bay leaf

a few sprigs of thyme

5 black peppercorns

about 1 teaspoon cornflour (optional)

FOR THE BRAISED SALSIFY

6–8 salsify stalks, peeled

a good knob of butter

1 tablespoon chopped parsley

Preheat the oven to 220°C/gas 7. Season the ribs with salt and pepper and dust with 1 tablespoon of the flour. Place them in a roasting tray with the onions, celery and carrot, and roast in the oven for 30–40 minutes, turning the ribs every so often, until nicely browned.

Transfer the vegetables and ribs to a heavy-based saucepan, leaving any fat in the pan. Add the rest of the flour and tomato purée to the roasting pan and stir over a low heat on the hob for a minute. Gradually add the beer and beef stock, stirring well to avoid lumps forming. Bring to the boil, then pour over the ribs and vegetables in the pan.

Add the garlic, bay leaf, thyme sprigs, peppercorns and a good pinch of salt. Cover and simmer gently for 1½–2 hours or until the meat is tender. Check it by removing a piece from the pot; it should be almost falling off the bone without being too soft.

Lift out the beef short ribs and set aside; discard the vegetables. Return the sauce to the heat and let bubble until it has reduced and thickened to a rich gravy-like consistency. If it's not thick enough, mix the cornflour to a paste with a little water, stir into the sauce and simmer for a few minutes, stirring. Strain the sauce and return the beef ribs to the pan.

Cut the salsify on the diagonal into 2–3cm pieces. Add to a saucepan of salted water, bring to the boil and simmer for 6–8 minutes until tender. Drain and toss with the butter and chopped parsley in a warm serving dish. Season with salt and pepper to taste.

To serve, reheat the beef ribs in the sauce, then divide among warm shallow bowls. Serve with the braised salsify and bashed neeps (buttery mashed turnips or swede).

OX CHEEK AND STOUT PIE *serves 4–6*

You will probably need to ask your butcher in advance for ox cheeks, or you could use beef flank, feather blade or shin instead for this pie. Trying to be a bit clever here, I've used a piece of scooped-out bone marrow as the pie funnel, but you don't need to go to that much trouble, you could just use a normal pie funnel.

1kg ox cheeks, trimmed

2 tablespoons plain flour

salt and freshly ground black pepper

2 tablespoons vegetable oil

25g butter

a piece of bone marrow long enough to act as a pie funnel, marrow scooped out and reserved (optional)

1 small onion, peeled and finely chopped

1 garlic clove, peeled and crushed

1 teaspoon tomato purée

250ml stout

1.5 litres beef stock (or a good beef stock cube dissolved in this amount of hot water)

1 teaspoon chopped thyme

1 bay leaf

about 1 teaspoon cornflour (optional)

FOR THE PASTRY

225g self-raising flour

1 teaspoon salt

85g shredded beef suet

60g butter, chilled and coarsely grated

about 150ml cold water

plain flour for dusting

1 medium egg, beaten, to glaze

Cut the ox cheeks into even 3–4cm pieces. Season ½ tablespoon of the flour with salt and pepper and lightly flour the meat. Heat the oil in a heavy-based frying pan and fry the meat in two or three batches over a high heat until nicely browned. Remove and set aside.

Heat the butter in a large heavy-based saucepan, with the scooped out marrow if using, and gently fry the onion and garlic for a few minutes until softened. Add the remaining flour and the tomato purée, and stir over a low heat for a minute. Slowly add the stout, stirring constantly to avoid lumps forming. Bring to the boil and simmer until the liquor has reduced by half.

Stir in the beef stock, then add the pieces of meat, thyme and bay leaf. Bring to a simmer, cover with a lid and simmer very gently for about 2 hours until the meat is tender. (Alternatively, you could cook it in a low oven at 160°C/gas 3.) It's difficult to be precise with braising meats, sometimes an extra half an hour may be needed. The best way to check is by tasting the meat.

When the meat is cooked, the sauce should have thickened to a gravy-like consistency. If not, mix the cornflour to a paste with a little water, stir into the sauce and simmer for a few minutes, stirring.

Let the mixture cool down, then use to fill a pie dish to approximately 1cm from the rim of the dish. Place the piece of hollowed-out bone marrow or a pie funnel in the centre.

To make the pastry, in a large bowl, combine the flour and salt, then mix in the shredded suet and grated butter. Make a well in the middle and add the water, mixing with a round-bladed knife to a smooth dough. If necessary, add an extra tablespoon or two of water. Knead the dough for a minute.

Roll out the pastry on a lightly floured surface to a 7mm thickness, the shape of your pie dish (round or oval). Trim the pastry to about 2cm larger than the pie dish all round. Brush the pastry edges with a little of the beaten egg.

Lift the pastry over your rolling pin and lay it, egg-washed edges down, over the pie. Cut a slit or hole in the middle for the bone marrow or pie funnel to poke through and press the pastry edges onto the rim of the dish. Brush the pastry all over with beaten egg. You can decorate it with leaves or other shapes cut from the leftover pastry if you wish, glazing these too with eggwash. Leave to rest in a cool place for 30 minutes.

Preheat the oven to 200°C/gas 6. Bake the pie for 40–50 minutes until the pastry is golden. Serve with a selection of winter vegetables.

OXTAIL SALAD *serves 4–6*

Braised oxtail may not be the obvious choice for a salad but I've often made this when I've had some braised oxtail leftover from a dinner. It can be served in summer or winter – you just need to change the salad vegetables according to the season.

FOR THE BRAISED OXTAIL

1.kg oxtail, cut into 2–3cm thick pieces and trimmed of excess fat

salt and freshly ground black pepper

50g plain flour, plus extra for dusting

60g butter, plus extra for the carrots

1 onion, peeled and finely chopped

2 garlic cloves, peeled and crushed

1 teaspoon thyme leaves

2 teaspoons tomato purée

100ml red wine

2 litres beef stock (or a couple of good stock cubes, dissolved in the same amount of hot water)

FOR THE SALAD

handful of small salad and herb leaves, such as purslane, watercress, chervil and chives

1 carrot, peeled

1 turnip, peeled

FOR THE DRESSING

1 tablespoon cider vinegar

½ teaspoon English mustard

3 tablespoons extra virgin rapeseed oil

First braise the oxtail. Preheat the oven to 220°C/gas 7. Season the pieces of oxtail and dust them lightly with flour. Place in a roasting tray and roast in the oven for 30 minutes, turning them halfway through to make sure they are nicely coloured on both sides.

Heat the 60g butter in large heavy-based saucepan and gently cook the onion with the garlic and thyme for 3–4 minutes until softened, stirring every so often. Add the flour and tomato purée and stir well. Gradually pour in the wine and stock, stirring well to avoid lumps forming, and bring to the boil.

Add the pieces of oxtail, then lower the heat, cover and simmer very gently for about 2 hours. Check the pieces of oxtail: the meat should be tender and easily removed from the bone; if not, replace the lid and cook for another 15 minutes or so.

Meanwhile, for the dressing, whisk the ingredients together in a bowl and season with salt and pepper to taste. Wash the salad leaves and pat dry. Shred the carrot and turnip into very fine matchsticks.

Drain the oxtail in a colander over a bowl to reserve the sauce. When the oxtail is cool enough to handle, take the meat off the bone in bite-sized pieces and place in a saucepan with a little of the sauce.

Toss the salad leaves, carrot and turnip with the dressing and arrange in the centre of individual serving plates. Reheat the oxtail a little and spoon around the salad, with a small amount of sauce just coating the meat. Spoon any remaining dressing over the oxtail.

December

Small, tender GAME BIRDS, BRUSSELS SPROUTS *and their leafy tops,* PARSNIPS, *knobbly* JERUSALEM ARTICHOKES and *native* NUTS *for the festive season...*

OTHER INGREDIENTS NOT TO BE MISSED

Mutton   Goose   Turkey   Pheasant   Herring   Salsify   Swede   Watercress

Chanterelles   Wood blewits   Sea purslane   Alexanders   Sea beet   Three cornered garlic

Quince   Forced rhubarb

December arrives and, if you haven't already had that pre-Christmas organisational rush of blood to the head, it's time to starts panicking. The festive period is only weeks away, so it's time to decide where to go, what to cook and what presents to buy… unless, of course, like me you prefer to leave everything to the last minute.

I see December as a month for celebrating the near-end to the glorious British game season and making the most of it with pies, soups and hotpots, as well as roasting the birds that are still in their prime. A couple of years ago I was, as usual, entertaining at home on Christmas day – no one ever invites me for dinner so I have no choice in the matter!

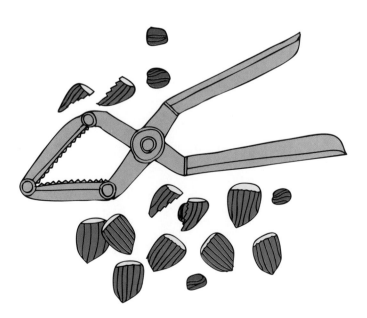

I decided to do a game feast for the main course so I bought lots of small game birds like snipe, teal, partridge, woodcock, widgeon, etc. It was a great success and a real talking point among guests, so I've carried on the tradition, I mean who ever recites a turkey lunch? Now that would be talking turkey…

The problem is that the flavour of turkey has nothing on game, or goose for that matter. These simply roasted tiny birds all have unique flavours of their own so you can have a whole one, half of one, share the larger ones with your partner and have a right old feast. I serve them with a jelly, often quince, and some simple greens like sprout tops and, of course, parsnip crisps and bread sauce. My guests normally follow my lead and eat the birds using their hands, even getting stuck into the brains of snipe and woodcock – the two birds that traditionally get trussed with their long pointed beaks.

All of the ingredients featured this month can most certainly make an appearance on the Christmas dinner table. Brussels sprouts and parsnips are classic accompaniments, obviously, but you can do so much more with them. If you're a gardener you may well appreciate sprout tops and their leaves, which make a tasty alternative to greens or cabbage. A few greengrocers are now seeing the gap in the market for sprout tops, so keep a look out for them, or visit your local farmers' market where you should hopefully find some. And don't give up on the chance of finding wild mushrooms this late on. Last year, I was picking chanterelles in Epping forest in mid-December and they kept right up until Christmas day when I served them tossed in with my sprout tops.

This month is also prime time for roots and tubers – parsnips, swede and carrots naturally, but also my favourite Jerusalem artichokes, which can hold their own as a stand-alone vegetable. Their faintly perfumed, nutty, earthy flavour is a foil for even the most delicate of ingredients. In this respect, they are like a potato with fewer carbs, but the sad thing is that there are not so many farmers growing them.

Root vegetables have an honest flavour about them, totally down to earth and not in any way pretentious. We tend to cook them simply as an accompaniment to serve alongside roasts and alike, but they offer so many culinary possibilities – in soups, stews, hotpots, even salads. I reckon that roots never get used to their full potential – something as simple as a bunch of carrots or parsnips can make a lovely, warming winter soup, especially when you add a little spice.

If you've been squirrel-like and saving up your nuts then you can have some fun, roasting, stuffing and even dipping our native nuts in chocolate for the festive period. They have many uses in the kitchen beyond being cracked at Christmas and making a mess all over the floor and down the sides of the sofa.

In fact nuts play a big part in cooking, especially in desserts and cakes. Foreign nuts like almonds, macadamias, pecans and pine nuts may seem more of a luxurious eating option than our homegrown nuts, but I reckon that's just down to fashion and what we are tempted to nibble on with pre-dinner drinks in restaurants and bars. Basically whatever recipe you come across with a foreign nut, you can more than likely use a British alternative.

Small game birds

The fun of eating game birds is that they each have their own unique flavour. The whole process is a bit of a ceremony, those delicious accompaniments like the bread sauce, jellies and game chips (parsnip crisps) just make it a unique dining experience. The smaller of the game birds tend to be harder to come by. The likes of woodcock and snipe are crafty and their zigzag takeoff makes it difficult sport even for the best shots. So understandably, these little birds come with a high price tag and may not seem good value for money at game dealers alongside their more meaty cousins ... but believe me they are worth every penny.

CHRISTMAS LUNCH OF SMALL GAME BIRDS *serves 8*

Game birds like teal, snipe, woodcock, widgeon, pintail and even pigeon are a great way to entertain your guests at Christmas. What's more they don't take much longer than 15 minutes in a hot oven to cook so you can pop them in while you are having your starter.

If you are keen with a shotgun, you can save up these less common birds in the freezer during the season and pull them out on the 24th for your game bird feast. You should allow a couple of birds per person for a really unusual Christmas day treat.

You can buy your birds trussed or tied, or just as they are, and if you're using snipe and woodcock then the beak can be used to truss the birds through the legs for an even more dramatic presentation.

If your birds come with the livers, these can be fried quickly and spread onto toast. I'd also recommend serving a pan gravy or a jelly, such as cranberry, rowan, quince or rose hip.

> 16 or so small game birds (see above)
> salt and freshly ground black pepper
> 32 sage leaves
> a few knobs of butter, softened
> TO SERVE
> pan gravy or a hedgerow jelly (see above)
> bread sauce (see page 217)

Preheat the oven to 230°C/gas 8. Season the birds inside and out and place the sage leaves in the cavities. Rub the breasts with the softened butter. Place in one or two large roasting trays and roast for about 15 minutes, keeping them pink and basting with the butter from time to time. If you are cooking widgeon, allow an extra 10 minutes or so, as they tend to be twice the size.

Serve the game birds on wooden boards or a platter, with pan gravy or a hedgerow jelly. Buttered sprout tops tossed with chanterelles or lightly roasted chestnuts work a treat and bread sauce is a must.

top for the lid and carefully hollow out the flesh from the potato, using a small sharp knife, a grapefruit knife or melon baller, leaving about a 1cm shell of potato. (You can cook and mash up the potato to serve with the snipe or simply season and butter the pieces and roast with a little chopped onion and bacon while the snipe is cooking.)

Put a knob of butter in the bottom of the potato, place the seasoned snipe on top, then the rest of the butter on top with the sage and thyme. Replace the lid and bake for about an hour. Serve immediately.

SMOOTH WOODCOCK PÂTÉ *serves 4–6*

This is a nostalgic dish for me, as it takes me back to my early days at Grosvenor House in London, where a rich, silky smooth woodcock pâté – well, more of a mousse really – was on the menu. It was a bugger to make, involving lots of reductions of meat liquid, as well as forcing the mixture through a sieve to ensure a fine texture. I thought I should share it with you, though I've shortened the laborious process so it won't drive you completely mad. If you can't get your hands on a woodcock, you could use partridge, pigeon or pheasant – even a mixture of game birds will do. Sometimes good game dealers have birds that are not in perfect condition for roasting though still fine to eat, and these would be ideal here.

2–3 woodcock

½ glass of white wine

½ glass of red wine

50ml Madeira

50ml port

2 tablespoons brandy

a little vegetable oil

3 large shallots, peeled and roughly chopped

1 litre chicken stock (or a good stock cube dissolved in this amount of boiling water)

2 garlic cloves, peeled and crushed

a few sprigs of thyme

4 juniper berries

salt and freshly ground black pepper

a couple of good knobs of butter

100g duck or chicken livers

100ml double cream

SNIPE 'BUTCHER'S TREAT' *serves 4*

Whenever I'm up at Ben and Silvy Weatheralls' in Dumfriesshire, I'm always inspired by something to do with game, however simple or complicated it may be. What I did learn from my last eventful few days in the Highlands was a new way to cook snipe. Ben recited a recipe from a book by Prue Coates, *Prue's New Country Cooking*, which sounded just genius. Here's my adaptation.

A snipe, as you may well know, doesn't have a lot of meat on the bone so this sounded like a great idea and a fun way to serve any of these tiny game birds.

4 oven-ready snipe

salt and freshly ground black pepper

4 large baking potatoes

a couple of good knobs of butter

4 sage leaves

a few sprigs of thyme

Preheat the oven to 230°C/gas 8. Season the snipe with salt and pepper.

Cut a small slice off a long side of the potato so that it can sit level on this base. Cut about a 1cm slice off the

Remove the legs from the woodcock, and then cut through the leg joint to separate the thigh from the drumstick. Put the drumsticks to one side. Remove the skin from the thighs and cut out the bone with the point of a sharp knife. Cut the breasts away from the carcass and remove the skin.

Cut the thigh and breast meat into rough 2cm chunks and place in a bowl with the wine, Madeira, port and brandy. Leave to marinate in the fridge for 24 hours.

Meanwhile, chop the drumsticks and carcass into small pieces using a heavy chopping knife or cleaver. Heat a little oil in a heavy-based saucepan and fry the bones and shallots, stirring well, until they are nicely coloured. Add the chicken stock, garlic, thyme and juniper. Bring to the boil, lower the heat and simmer for an hour.

Strain the stock through a fine sieve into a clean pan. Add the marinating liquor from the woodcock and boil until reduced to about 2 or 3 spoonfuls of syrupy liquid.

Dry the pieces of meat on some kitchen paper and season with salt and pepper. Heat half of the butter in a frying pan and cook the meat over a medium heat for 3–4 minutes, stirring every so often and keeping it pink. Put to one side.

Add the rest of the butter to the pan, season the livers and sauté them for 2–3 minutes, stirring and keeping them pink. Mix the woodcock, livers and reduced stock together. Now purée the mixture in a blender or food processor, in two or three batches to keep it as smooth as possible. You will need to stop every so often during blending to scrape down the sides with a spatula.

Whip the cream to a fairly stiff consistency and carefully fold into the mixture using a metal spoon. Transfer to a serving dish or container, cover with cling film and refrigerate overnight.

Serve the pâté simply with toast and a salad of small leaves on the side.

BREAD SAUCE *serves* 4

This is a useful sauce to serve with any simply cooked game birds. For a full flavour, infuse the milk with the onion, bay leaf and spices a day ahead.

1 small onion, peeled and halved

50g butter

3 cloves

1 bay leaf

500ml milk

pinch of freshly grated nutmeg

salt and freshly ground black pepper

100g fresh white breadcrumbs

Finely chop one half of the onion and cook it gently in half the butter until soft. Stud the other onion half with the cloves, pushing them through the bay leaf to anchor it. Put the milk, nutmeg and studded onion in the saucepan with the cooked onion and bring to the boil. Season with salt and pepper and simmer for 10–15 minutes. Take off the heat and leave to infuse for at least 30 minutes.

To finish the sauce, discard the studded onion, then add the breadcrumbs and return to a low heat. Simmer gently for 10 minutes, giving the sauce an occasional stir. Tip a quarter of the sauce into a blender and process until smooth, then return to the pan and add the remaining 25g butter. Stir until the sauce is evenly combined, check the seasoning and keep warm until ready to serve.

Sprouts and sprout tops

By the time the festive period is over, most of us are pretty bored with Brussels sprouts, but there's more to sprouts than just boiling and tossing them in butter.

Leafy sprout tops have an excellent robust flavour and make a great, earthy accompaniment – either steamed or boiled and served on their own, or mixed with the sprouts themselves, or with other greens. I've recently discovered that they also make a great warm starter salad (see page 220).

For me, Brussels sprouts and their tops are an important part of a wintry bubble and squeak. Their flavour is so distinctive, whether you utilise leftovers or cook them freshly for the dish. Simply adapt my recipe for spring bubble and squeak (on page 79), replacing the broad beans and peas with chopped cooked sprouts.

SALAD OF SPROUT TOPS, SALSIFY AND HAM HOCK *serves 4 as a starter*

Blanched sprout tops make a tasty leaf for a warm salad starter. Alternatively, if you can't find these leafy tops, then the outer leaves from large Brussels sprouts will do. Salsify is another underused vegetable, which is hardly surprising given that it is a rather dirty-looking long, thin root. Once peeled, however, it has a totally unique eating quality.

1 small ham hock, cooked (see page 112), some of the cooking liquor reserved

6–7 salsify

juice of ½ lemon

salt and freshly ground black pepper

a couple of handfuls of sprout tops, thick stalks removed and washed

a little vegetable oil (optional)

FOR THE DRESSING

2 shallots, peeled, halved and finely chopped

1 tablespoon cider vinegar

1 tablespoon water

1 teaspoon English mustard

4 tablespoons extra virgin rapeseed oil

Have the ham hock cooked and ready with the reserved liquor.

For the salsify, have two bowls of water ready, one with the lemon juice added and the other for washing. Top, tail and half the salsify, then peel with a vegetable peeler, dipping them in the bowl of water as you're going, to ensure all the black skin is removed. As you've peeled each one, drop into the bowl of acidulated water.

For the dressing, put the shallots into a small pan with the cider vinegar and water and simmer until reduced by half, then remove from the heat and whisk in the mustard and oil. Season with salt and pepper to taste; set aside.

Add the salsify to a pan of well-salted water, bring to the boil and cook for 4–5 minutes until tender. Drain and leave to cool a little. Meanwhile, add the sprout tops to a pan of boiling salted water and cook for 3–4 minutes until tender, then drain.

Flake the ham hock into small pieces and reheat with a little of the cooking liquor, or pan-fry in a little oil until crisp if you prefer. Slice the salsify on the diagonal.

To serve, arrange the warm sprout tops and salsify on individual serving plates. Scatter the pieces of ham hock on top and spoon the dressing over.

CREAMED BRUSSELS SPROUTS *serves 4*

This is a really simple way to use up leftover sprouts, or to prepare them from fresh for that matter. It's a perfect match to roast game and poultry dishes, and a nice change to slot into the Christmas day lunch, although you may upset conservative in-laws.

1kg large Brussels sprouts, prepared and cooked

200ml double cream

salt and freshly ground black pepper

60g butter

Slice the cooked Brussels sprouts thinly. Bring the cream to a simmer in a saucepan and let bubble until reduced by half. Add the sliced sprouts and season with salt and pepper to taste. Simmer over a low heat for 4–5 minutes, stirring every so often. Add the butter and serve.

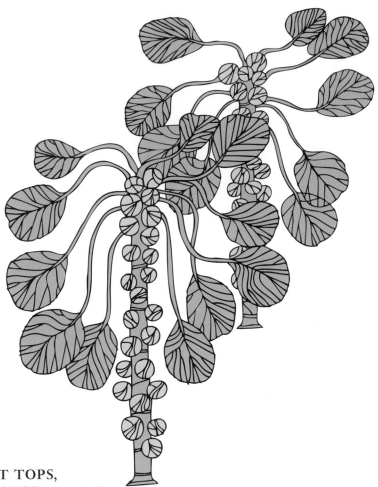

ROAST GOOSE WITH SPROUT TOPS, CHESTNUTS AND QUINCE SAUCE *serves 5–6*

I've tried lots of different ways of roasting a goose over the years and found that the legs need more time to cook, so putting them into the oven ahead of the breast makes sense. By roasting the bird this way, the breasts are cooked to medium, while the legs are slow-cooked and crispy. This process will also render plenty of fat from the goose to roast your spuds. The secret of a moist bird is to begin cooking it breast down, so that the skin fries in the hot fat released from under the skin.

If you have a larger gathering, of say 10–12 people, I'd suggest cooking two geese of this size, side by side, provided they'll fit in your oven.

1 goose, about 4–5kg

salt and freshly ground black pepper

20–30 chestnuts

1–1.2kg sprout tops, thick stalks removed and washed

a generous knob of butter

FOR THE QUINCE SAUCE

3–4 quince, peeled, quartered and cored

6 tablespoons caster sugar

50g butter

TO SERVE

poultry gravy (see right)

Preheat the oven to 160°C/gas 3. Remove the legs from the goose by pulling them away from the bone and cutting at the joint. Remove any fat and skin from underneath the bird on the backbone. Put the legs in a roasting tray in which they fit snugly and lay the fat on top or to the side of them. (The fat will render down to use for roast potatoes.) Season the duck legs and cook for 2½ hours, basting every so often. This can be done ahead.

Meanwhile, make the quince sauce. Put the quince into a pan, add water to cover and the sugar. Bring to the boil, lower the heat, then cover and simmer for about 40 minutes or until the quince is tender. Drain well. Mash the quince with the butter using a potato masher and keeping the sauce fairly chunky, or whiz in a blender if you'd rather it was smooth. Taste for sweetness and add a little more sugar if necessary, although the sauce shouldn't be too sweet to accompany goose.

When the duck legs are cooked, drain off and reserve the fat. Put the legs aside, ready to heat up 15 minutes before serving.

POULTRY GRAVY

It's always a good idea to get ahead by having gravy, or at least the basis for it, already made – especially at Christmas. With goose, or any poultry come to that, you'll never have enough giblets and neck to flavour your gravy, so bring in reinforcements. I'd recommend getting in some extra chicken wings, necks and bones. This recipe should make enough for Christmas Day, so scale up the quantities accordingly for extra batches to freeze.

500g chicken, goose or duck bones, or a mixture, chopped into small pieces, plus the giblets from the birds

1 large onion, peeled and roughly chopped

2 medium carrots, peeled and roughly chopped

1 celery stick, roughly chopped

1 leek, trimmed, roughly chopped and washed

2 garlic cloves, peeled and chopped

1 teaspoon tomato purée

1 tablespoon plain flour

2 litres chicken stock (or a good stock cube dissolved in this amount of hot water)

6 black peppercorns

a few sprigs of thyme

1 bay leaf

about 1 teaspoon cornflour (optional)

Preheat the oven to 200°C/gas 6. Put the poultry bones, giblets, chopped vegetables and garlic in a roasting tray and roast in the oven for about 15–20 minutes until lightly coloured, giving them a good stir every so often. When the bones are a nice golden brown colour, stir in the tomato purée, then the flour and stir well to mix with the bones and vegetables. Return to the oven for another 10 minutes.

Transfer the roasting tray from the oven to the hob. Add a little of the stock and stir over a low heat, scraping up the sediment from the bottom of the tray. This will start the thickening process.

Now tip everything into a large saucepan and pour on the rest of the stock. If the stock doesn't quite cover the bones, top up with some cold water. Add the peppercorns, thyme and bay leaf. Bring to the boil and skim off any scum from the surface. Lower the heat and simmer for 2 hours, topping up the liquor with boiling water as necessary to keep the ingredients covered. Skim occasionally as required.

Strain the gravy through a fine sieve into a clean pan and remove any fat from the surface with a ladle. Taste for strength and, if necessary, simmer to reduce and concentrate the flavour. If the gravy is not thick enough, mix the cornflour to a paste with a little water, stir into the gravy and simmer, stirring, for a few minutes.

For the goose itself, turn the oven up to 220°C/gas 7. Spoon a little of the rendered fat into a large roasting tray. Season the goose, then place breast side down in the tray. Roast for 45 minutes, draining off excess fat from the tray during cooking (adding it to the fat from the legs).

Now turn the bird over, so it is sitting upright and lower the oven setting to 200°C/gas 6. Roast for a further 30 minutes, putting the legs back in to reheat if you've cooked them in advance.

While the goose is roasting, cut a slit in each chestnut, place them on a baking tray and bake in the oven for about 10–15 minutes, being careful as they have a tendency to explode. Remove and leave until cool enough to handle, then carefully peel away the outer skin and rub off any brown skin. Cut the chestnuts in half.

When the goose is almost cooked, add the sprout tops to a pan of boiling salted water and cook for about 5–6 minutes or until tender. Drain, then toss with the butter and chestnuts. Season to taste.

Cut the goose breasts from the bone, using a sharp knife, and slice thinly. The leg meat can just be carved off the bone, or cut into chunks. Serve with the sprout tops and chestnuts, and potatoes roasted in the duck fat. Accompany with the quince sauce and gravy.

Parsnips

Parsnips are one of my favourite roots to use throughout the winter months. Not only are they incredibly tasty, they are also great value for money. In France, parsnips are fed to cattle, which is a complete waste of a great vegetable in my view.

They are such a versatile root – perfect for roasting, mashing and puréeing, they can also be sliced and baked with grated cheese and cream for a tasty vegetarian bake to accompany meaty and game dishes.

Parsnips also make delicious, nourishing soups – either flavourful broths packed with other vegetables too, or creamy soups with a subtle hint of spice. And for a tasty snack, its hard to beat deep-fried parsnips crisps (see below).

PARSNIP CRISPS WITH SEA SALT *serves 4–6*

These are my favourite of all vegetable crisps. They are great as snacks, or to serve as an accompaniment to game birds.

3 large parsnips, scrubbed clean

vegetable or corn oil for deep-frying

2 teaspoons sea salt

Top and tail the parsnips, leaving the skin on, unless it's very brown. Using a sharp mandolin (the Japanese ones are the best), slice the parsnips lengthways as thinly as possible, then dry the strips with a clean tea towel. If you don't possess a mandolin, use a swivel vegetable peeler instead.

Heat about an 8cm depth of vegetable oil in a deep-fat fryer or heavy-based saucepan to 180°C. Deep-fry the parsnip slices in the hot fat, a handful at a time, stirring occasionally to ensure that they don't stick together, for about 2–3 minutes until they colour.

As soon as they are ready, remove the parsnip crisps with a slotted spoon and drain on kitchen paper. Immediately season generously with the sea salt, crushing it in your fingers as you sprinkle it on. The parsnips may appear soft as you remove them from the oil, but once drained they will dry out and crisp up. Serve as soon as they are all cooked.

PARSNIP DROP SCONES WITH VENISON
AND JUNIPER SAUCE *serves* 4

These drop scones aren't traditional at all, I've just
made them up and found the sweetness of parsnip in this
format works a treat. I like to use the venison under-fillet
for dishes like this. It often gets sold with the saddle but
game dealers should be happy to part with it separately. If
time, marinate the venison in red wine with thyme sprigs,
crushed peppercorns, crushed juniper berries, and a little
oil in the fridge for 2–3 days, to improve the flavour.

4 venison under-fillets, each about 180g

vegetable oil for frying

salt and freshly ground black pepper

FOR THE PARSNIP DROP SCONES

1 large parsnip, about 200g

80g self-raising flour

1 medium egg, beaten

milk to mix

vegetable oil for frying

a good knob of butter

FOR THE JUNIPER SAUCE

a good knob of butter

2 medium shallots, peeled and finely
chopped

6 juniper berries, crushed

1 teaspoon plain flour

2 teaspoons redcurrant jelly

200ml beef stock (approximately)

For the drop scones, peel, halve and core the parsnip,
then chop roughly and cook in boiling salted water until
tender. Drain thoroughly and mash well. Put the mashed
parsnip into a bowl with the flour and beaten egg and mix
well, then stir in enough milk to make a stiff batter.
Season with salt and pepper.

Next make the sauce. Heat the butter in a pan and
gently cook the shallots and juniper berries for a couple
of minutes. Stir in the flour, then add the redcurrant jelly.
Now gradually stir in the hot stock to avoid lumps
forming. Bring to the boil, lower the heat and simmer

gently for about 10 minutes. Add a little more stock or water if the sauce is getting too thick and season with salt and pepper to taste.

Preheat the oven to 140°C/gas 1. To cook the drop scones, heat a little vegetable oil in a small non-stick omelette pan and ladle in enough batter to cover the bottom. (Or you could cook the drop scones two at a time in a larger frying pan.) Cook for 2–3 minutes on each side, adding a knob of butter as you turn them. Once they are nicely coloured and crisp, transfer to a warm plate and keep warm in the oven while you cook the rest, and the venison.

To cook the venison, heat a heavy-based frying pan with a little oil added. Season the fillets with salt and pepper and pan-fry them over a medium-high heat for 6–7 minutes, rolling them in the pan to get an even colour and keeping them nice and rare.

To serve, slice the venison fillets. Place a drop scone on each warm plate, arrange the venison on top and pour the juniper sauce over and around.

BAKED PARSNIPS WITH LANCASHIRE

serves 4–6

This is rather like a gratin dauphinoise, made with parsnips rather than potatoes. You could also try making it with turnips, or a mixture of parsnips and turnips if you like.

    750g parsnips
    400ml double cream
    400ml milk
    2 garlic cloves, peeled and crushed
    a good pinch of freshly grated nutmeg
    salt and freshly ground black pepper
    150g mature Lancashire cheese, freshly
    grated
    2 tablespoons fresh white breadcrumbs
    1 tablespoon chopped parsley

Preheat the oven to 190°C/gas 5. Peel the parsnips and cut them into rough 2–3cm chunks, cutting out the hard core. Pour the cream and milk into a pan and add the garlic, nutmeg, and some salt and pepper. Slowly bring to the boil, then remove from the heat and leave to cool a little.

Put the parsnips into an ovenproof gratin dish with all but 2 tablespoons of the grated cheese and mix well, then pour over the cream mixture.

Put the gratin dish into a roasting pan, then pour enough boiling water into the tin to come halfway up the side of the gratin dish. Bake in the oven for 1 hour or until the parsnips are cooked through; they may take a little longer.

Preheat the grill. Mix the breadcrumbs with the chopped parsley and the rest of the grated cheese and scatter over the gratin. Place under the grill for a few minutes until the topping is golden brown. Serve immediately, or cover with foil and leave in a low oven until ready to serve.

ROOT VEGETABLES WITH GOOSE FAT, GARLIC AND THYME *serves 4–6*

A wintry selection of root vegetables is a great accompaniment to almost any main course you might concoct, even fish dishes. In a mixture like this, the roots work in perfect harmony. Here I've used the obvious ones, but you could add salsify, or possibly kohlrabi – that alien-looking vegetable with a turnipy-radish taste.

    12 garlic cloves, left in their skins
    2–3 tablespoons goose or duck fat
    2 medium parsnips, peeled
    1 small swede, peeled
    2 medium-large turnips
    salt and freshly ground black pepper
    a few sprigs of thyme
    1 tablespoon chopped parsley

Preheat the oven to 180°C/gas 4. Put the garlic cloves into a large roasting tray with the goose fat and cook for about 30 minutes until they soften, turning occasionally.

Meanwhile, halve the parsnips and cut out the cores. Cut all the root vegetables into rough 1cm cubes. Bring a pan of boiling salted water to the boil and blanch the vegetables for 2–3 minutes, then drain.

Add the blanched root veg to the garlic in the roasting tray along with the thyme. Season generously and roast for about 15–20 minutes, turning every so often, until the vegetables are lightly coloured and tender. Stir in the chopped parsley and serve.

Jerusalem artichokes

The appearance of these knobbly tubers can be a bit off-putting, but once you get them into the kitchen they can be treated like most other roots and tubers – roasted, mashed, puréed, even fried. In their simplest form – boiled or steamed and tossed in butter – they are a delicious versatile accompaniment. Or you can purée them after cooking with a splash of cream to serve with roast and grilled meats, especially lamb.

You can also slice Jerusalem artichokes wafer-thin and deep-fry the slices to make crisps, in the same way as parsnips (see page 225). Or use them in place of potatoes to make a creamy gratin Dauphinoise.

Peeling the uneven tubers can be rather a test of patience, so allow yourself plenty of time for this.

JERUSALEM ARTICHOKE SOUP *serves 4–6*

This is one of the easiest soups to make and I've found the flavour to be pretty consistent every time I've made it. Finish with an extra spoonful of cream if you like, and perhaps a sprinkling of chopped herbs.

a good knob of butter

1 medium onion, peeled and roughly chopped

1 leek, trimmed, roughly chopped and washed

500g Jerusalem artichokes, peeled and cut into quarters

1.5 litres vegetable stock

salt and freshly ground white pepper

2 tablespoons double cream

Melt the butter in a saucepan and gently cook the onion and leek until soft. Add the Jerusalem artichokes and the vegetable stock and season lightly with salt and pepper. Bring to the boil, lower the heat and simmer for about 25 minutes until the artichokes are tender. Strain about a quarter of the stock into a jug and set aside.

Whiz the rest of the soup in a blender until smooth, then strain through a fine sieve into a pan. Stir in as much of the reserved stock as you need to get the right texture. Stir in the cream, check the seasoning and serve.

ROASTED JERUSALEM ARTICHOKES AND SHALLOTS WITH ROSEMARY *serves 4*

When you roast a Jerusalem artichoke, its flavour becomes concentrated and it seems to take on a different character. Shallots, roasted in their skins, are the perfect partner and a handful of rosemary added towards the end of cooking just gives them another dimension. This is an excellent accompaniment to grilled or roast lamb.

12 large shallots

500g Jerusalem artichokes, scrubbed

2–3 tablespoons extra virgin rapeseed oil

salt and freshly ground black pepper

a few sprigs of rosemary

a couple good knobs of butter

Preheat the oven to 180°C/Gas 4. Lay the shallots on a baking tray and roast them in their skins for about 45–50 minutes until tender. Remove from the oven and leave until cool enough to handle.

Meanwhile, toss the Jerusalem artichokes in the rapeseed oil in a roasting tray and season with salt and pepper. Bake for about 30–40 minutes, turning them every so often until almost tender.

Pop the shallots out of their skins by cutting a sliver off the root end and pushing them out. Toss the shallots and rosemary in with the artichokes and bake for 15 minutes, turning them occasionally. Transfer to a serving dish, add the butter and toss to mix, then serve.

SCALLOPS WITH BLACK PUDDING AND JERUSALEM ARTICHOKE PURÉE *serves 4*

The sweetness of freshly shucked scallops really works well with the earthiness of Jerusalem artichokes. If you're not confident about opening scallops yourself, then ask your fishmonger to do it for you. Don't be tempted to buy those ready-prepared ones, unless you know that they have been freshly shucked; more often than not, they will have been soaked in water, frozen or washed to death and have practically no flavour left.

300g Jerusalem artichokes

salt and freshly ground black pepper

80g butter

150g good quality black pudding

1 tablespoon rapeseed or vegetable oil

12 medium scallops, cleaned and trimmed

a handful of picked parsley

Peel the Jerusalem artichokes and cut them in half if large. Add to a pan of salted water, bring to the boil and simmer for 10–15 minutes or until tender. Drain well and whiz in a blender or food processor to a purée.

Return to a clean pan and place over a low heat. Warm the purée for a few minutes, stirring so it doesn't stick, until it has reduced slightly to a spoonable consistency; it shouldn't be wet and sloppy. Season with salt and pepper to taste and stir in about 30g of the butter; keep warm.

Cut the black pudding into small nuggets and set aside ready to cook.

Rub a non-stick heavy-based frying pan with the tiniest amount of oil (too much will make the scallops boil rather than fry). Heat until almost smoking, then add the scallops and cook over a medium-high heat for a minute on each side. Immediately remove from the pan to avoid overcooking and place on a plate; keep warm.

Lower the heat and add the black pudding, parsley and the rest of the butter to the pan. Cook gently for 2–3 minutes to warm through, stirring every so often.

To serve, spoon the Jerusalem artichoke purée onto warm serving plates, place the scallops on top, then spoon the butter and black pudding over.

Nuts

These are a useful storecupboard standby in the kitchen for all sorts of sweet and savoury dishes. They lend flavour and texture to cakes, teabreads, biscuits, meringue desserts, steamed puddings and crumble toppings.

Nuts, such as hazelnuts and walnuts, are delicious simply toasted with a little oil and sea salt and scattered into a salad, or even tossed into vegetables like greens and spinach. And when they are in season, it's great to have a bowl of fresh nuts alongside the fruit bowl to snack on.

ROAST PHEASANT WITH CHESTNUT DUMPLINGS *serves* 4

Pheasant has a tendency to overcook and dry out before you know it, but there is a way of avoiding this. By removing the breasts, wrapping them in caul fat and using the thighs, chestnuts and herbs to make dumplings, you end up with a succulent dish, instead of dry, tough meat.

2 plump pheasants

2 teaspoons plain flour for dusting

a little vegetable oil for roasting

1 onion, peeled and roughly chopped

1 carrot, peeled and roughly chopped

60ml cider

1 litre chicken or beef stock

a few sprigs of thyme

4 juniper berries

salt and freshly ground black pepper

caul fat for wrapping

FOR THE DUMPLINGS

16–18 lightly roasted and shelled (or vacuum-packed cooked) chestnuts

25g butter

2 shallots, peeled and finely chopped

1 teaspoon chopped thyme leaves

40g fresh white breadcrumbs

1 tablespoon chopped parsley

Preheat the oven to 200°C/gas 6. Carefully remove the breasts from the pheasants and set aside. Bone the thighs and finely chop or mince the meat. Chop the thigh bones and drumsticks, dust with the flour and place in an oiled roasting tray with the onion and carrot. Roast for about 20–30 minutes, stirring every so often until the bones are lightly browned.

Transfer the roasted bones and vegetables to a saucepan. Gradually stir in the cider and chicken stock, then add the thyme and juniper berries. Bring to the boil, lower the heat and simmer gently for about 40 minutes.

To make the dumplings, roughly chop the chestnuts. Melt the butter in a small pan and gently cook the shallots with the chopped thyme for 2–3 minutes until softened. Transfer to a bowl. Add the chopped or minced thigh meat, chestnuts, breadcrumbs and parsley. Season with salt and pepper and mix well. Divide into four portions and shape into balls, then carefully wrap them in a couple of layers of caul fat.

Season the pheasant breasts and wrap them in a single layer of caul fat. Heat a little oil in a medium roasting tray in the oven, then add the dumplings and roast for about 15–20 minutes, turning them every so often. Add the pheasant breasts and roast for about 4–5 minutes on each side, keeping them nice and pink. (Don't be tempted to leave them in the oven to keep warm while you prepare everything else.)

Meanwhile, strain the sauce through a fine sieve into a clean pan and simmer over a medium heat until reduced and thickened to the desired consistency.

To serve, cut the pheasant breasts in half and arrange on warm plates with the dumplings. Pour the sauce over and serve with vegetables of your choice.

CHOCOLATE-DIPPED WALNUTS

makes about 48 *pieces*

These make perfect little Christmas treats to have with coffee or a tipple of Armagnac or Cognac. They are simple to prepare and can be made about a week ahead. Like all good things, they rely on the best ingredients – ideally freshly shelled walnuts, good dark chocolate and the finest cocoa powder.

> 24 walnuts in the shell or 150g good
> quality shelled walnuts
> 200g good quality dark chocolate
> 60–70g good quality cocoa powder

Shell the walnuts if you've bought them in their shells. Break the chocolate into a heatproof bowl and place over a pan of simmering water until melted. Sift the cocoa powder onto a shallow tray and have another tray ready.

Dip the walnuts into the melted chocolate a few at a time, then remove with a fork, tapping it on the side of the bowl to encourage the excess chocolate to run back into the bowl. Now drop them into the cocoa, turning the walnuts with a clean fork and shaking the tray so they are well coated, then place on the clean tray. Repeat with the rest of the walnuts.

Store the coated nuts in an airtight container in a cool place and use within a week.

CHRISTMAS MESS *serves* 8

Cranberries, in the form of a sauce or jelly, are synonymous with Christmas dinner, though these tart red berries are worthy of more than being just an adjunct to the turkey. Like chestnuts, they lend themselves to a host of savoury dishes and interesting desserts, such as this lovely meringue concoction, which is loosely based on an Italian *monte bianco*.

You don't need to go to the trouble of making fresh meringues unless you really want to, there are plenty of good ready-made meringues on the market that are suitable for this dish.

> 40–50 chestnuts
> 2 tablespoons icing sugar
> 500ml double cream
> 80g caster sugar
> 150–200g cooked meringue
> FOR THE CRANBERRY SAUCE
> 200g fresh cranberries
> 90g sugar
> 1 small cinnamon stick
> juice of 1 orange

Preheat the oven to 200°C/gas 6. Make an incision in the top of each chestnut with a small sharp knife and place them on a baking tray. Bake in the oven for about 20 minutes, then remove and leave to cool.

Meanwhile for the sauce, put the cranberries, sugar and cinnamon into a heavy-based saucepan with the orange juice. Stir over a low heat until the sugar has dissolved, then simmer gently for about 20–25 minutes until the cranberries have softened. Discard the cinnamon. Taste the sauce for sweetness and add a little more sugar if necessary. Leave to cool.

Peel the chestnuts, removing as much of the brown skin as you possibly can. Place the nuts on a foil-lined baking tray and dust with the icing sugar. Bake in the oven for about 20 minutes, turning the chestnuts every so often. Remove and set aside to cool.

Whip the cream and caster sugar together in a bowl until very thick, using an electric whisk if you wish.

To assemble, break the meringue into pieces and fold into the cream with about two-thirds of the cold cranberry sauce and two-thirds of the chestnuts. Pile onto the centre of individual serving plates. Scatter the remaining chestnuts on top and spoon the rest of the cranberry sauce over. Serve at once.

Index

Acknowledgements

My sincere thanks to those who have worked on this book: Jason Lowe
for his superb photography; Marcus Oakley for his original, witty
illustrations; Janet Illsley for her work on the text; Lawrence Morton for
his immaculate design; and Jane O'Shea, Publishing Director at Quadrille.
I am also grateful to all my suppliers and food producers who are always a
source of inspiration. Last but not least, a special thank you to Clare Lattin
for her constant support… and for putting up with me working all hours.